Sheffield Hallam University
Learning and IT Services
Collegiate Learning Centre
Collegiate Crescent Campus
Sheffield   S10 2BP

101 972 228 2

Sheffield Hallam University
Learning and Information Services
Withdrawn From S

comparative

'E WEEK LOAN

KT-446-031

```
compact
criminology
```

Series editors: Nicole Rafter and Paul Rock

Compact Criminology is an exciting new series that invigorates and challenges the international field of criminology.

Books in the series are short, authoritative, innovative assessments of emerging issues in criminology and criminal justice – offering critical, accessible introductions to important topics. They take a global rather than a narrowly national approach. Eminently readable and first-rate in quality, each book is written by a leading specialist.

Compact Criminology provides a new type of tool for teaching and research, one that is flexible and light on its feet. The series is designed to address fundamental needs in the growing and increasingly differentiated field of criminology.

Other *Compact Criminology* titles include:

Comparing Criminal Justice by David Nelken
Crime and Risk by Pat O'Malley
Crime and Terrorism by Peter Grabosky and Michael Stohl
Experimental Criminology by Lawrence Sherman

Compact Criminology International Advisory Board:

Jan van Dijk, Tilburg University
Peter Grabosky, Australian National University
Kelly Hannah-Moffat, University of Toronto
John Laub, University of Maryland
Alison Liebling, University of Cambridge

comparative criminal justice
making sense of difference

David Nelken

Los Angeles | London | New Delhi
Singapore | Washington DC

© David Nelken 2010

First published 2010

Apart from any fair dealing for the purposes of research
or private study, or criticism or review, as permitted
under the Copyright, Designs and Patents Act, 1988, this
publication may be reproduced, stored or transmitted in any
form, or by any means, only with the prior permission in
writing of the publishers, or in the case of reprographic
reproduction, in accordance with the terms of licences
issued by the Copyright Licensing Agency. Enquiries
concerning reproduction outside those terms should be
sent to the publishers.

SAGE Publications Ltd
1 Oliver's Yard
55 City Road
London EC1Y 1SP

SAGE Publications Inc.
2455 Teller Road
Thousand Oaks, California 91320

SAGE Publications India Pvt Ltd
B 1/I 1 Mohan Cooperative Industrial Area
Mathura Road, New Delhi 110 044
India

SAGE Publications Asia-Pacific Pte Ltd
33 Pekin Street #02-01
Far East Square
Singapore 048763

Library of Congress Control Number Available

British Library Cataloguing in Publication data

A catalogue record for this book is available from the British Library

ISBN 978-1-84787-936-3 (hbk)
ISBN 978-1-84787-937-0 (pbk)

Typeset by C&M Digitals (P) Ltd, Chennai, India
Printed by CPI Antony Rowe, Chippenham, Wiltshire
Printed on paper from sustainable resources

FSC
www.fsc.org
MIX
Paper from
responsible sources
FSC® C013604

SHEFFIELD HALLAM UNIVERSITY
WL
345.05
NE
COLLEGIATE LEARNING CENTRE

We have to know what we are doing, protecting an order that doesn't exist, to make a security that cannot exist ... it is not possible to change anything until you understand the substance you wish to change ... to change something you do not understand is the true nature of evil. (Winterson 1991: 93, 138)

contents

acknowledgements

I should like to thank Nicole Rafter and Paul Rock for inviting me to contribute to this series and for their valuable editorial comments; Paul Roberts also offered valuable observations on the manuscript. Thanks also to Caroline Porter, Sarah-Jayne Boyd and others at Sage for all their advice and support. For anything I may have learned about this subject I owe particular thanks to my Italian friends, colleagues and students. But for the encouragement of my friends Malcolm Feeley and Stuart Scheingold I might not have come to write this book. Without Matilde and my family I could not have written it. It is dedicated to the memory of Dino Betti, *partigiano and maestro*.

introduction: changing paradigms

Comparative criminal justice is the study of what people and institutions in different places do – and should do – about crime problems. More broadly, it looks for links between crime, social order and punishment, and explores the role played by police, prosecutors, courts, prisons and other actors and institutions in the wider context of various forms of social control. In this opening chapter I describe how established undergraduate USA textbooks deal with these issues and contrast this with the types of work found in journals, edited collections and monographs which provide evidence of the paradigm change that this area of enquiry is currently undergoing.

There is little need to insist on the wider relevance of this subject. It is impossible to open a newspaper, watch television or check the internet without coming across matters that involve comparative criminal justice. There are still very real differences worldwide in what is seen as the proper role of criminal law, in resort to criminal justice systems as compared to other forms of sanctioning, in the political independence of the legal system, in the behaviour of police, the powers of prosecutors, lay or expert involvement, the rights of victims, the use of prison or the death penalty, or the extent of 'trial by media'. Such contrasts give rise to difficult political and policy questions. What is to be done – if anything – about what seem like barbaric practices in far away places? Can a society borrow reforms successfully from other places? The media in Western countries tend to magnify news of differences from and in the Islamic world. But there are also puzzling differences nearer among Western countries. How can we explain why incarceration rates in the USA are six to seven times as high as in most European countries – will the use of prison elsewhere follow this lead?

Why, for example, in 2008 did criminal court judges in Italy appeal to the United Nations to save them from the attacks of Prime Minister Berlusconi? Whatever answers are offered are likely to touch on genuine specificities about the current role of courts and prisons in these countries as compared to others.

As these examples also testify, however, it is getting difficult to distinguish what goes on 'here' from what goes on 'there'. In many countries crime is attributed to the growth of immigration – indeed, in Continental Europe unauthorised migration has itself been turned into a crime that ends up occupying much of the ordinary work of the lower courts. The obsession with crime and punishment, in which a large part of the news media is increasingly taken up, not only worries us with criminality next door, but also (selectively) with that taking place in the rest of the global village. In the UK, when the tabloid *Sun* newspaper is unable to find a sufficiently shocking crime at home, so as to create alarm at home, it increasingly refers to events in foreign countries. But even the normally sober *Independent* newspaper carried a leader recently warning its readers:

> the forces of terror do not respect national boundaries. And those prepared to murder and die for a perverted interpretation of Islam are not easily identified. We need to wake up to the fact that we will never be able to safeguard Britain's streets totally so long as violent extremism has its base in Pakistan. (*Independent*, 11 April 2009)

At the same time, if crime threats come from abroad, so too do international institutions increasingly take on judicial or regulatory tasks.

If this were not enough of a challenge, there is more. There are also 'second-order' (and higher) comparative questions to be explored (Nelken, 2007a). In order to decide how (and how far) to harmonise what they do with what others do, comparing becomes an intrinsic part of the practical tasks of many of those crafting and administering criminal justice. Thus in order to study such processes we must also explore the way others make comparisons – which will often reveal the 'interested' interpretations of criminal justice practices by politicians, policy-makers, legal actors, journalists, activists, scholars and others.

Changing paradigms

The aim of this book is to give some idea of the benefits, difficulties and, hopefully, also the excitement, of systematic study of the workings of criminal justice in and across different places. But this is very much a field which is struggling to keep up with the changes it seeks to describe and explain. This can be seen if we turn to consider currently available (typically American) codified 'knowledge' of what comparative criminal justice has to offer. I do not propose to offer here a detailed exegesis of the various American textbooks in this subject, such as Reichel (2008), now in its fifth edition, or Dammer, Fairchild and Albanese (2005), Fields and Moore (2005), and Cole, Frankowski and Gertz (1987), and I take for granted the many positive features they each have as teaching tools for opening students' minds to other ways of doing things, which is their principal purpose. My comments have only to do with the type of theoretical approaches that they mobilise, the political assumptions they make, and the methodological problems they pass over.

In the choice between coverage and depth, most textbooks tend to give preference to the former. But in so far as they are often obliged to draw on official reports (or websites), this begs the question of the reliability and validity of the sources chosen. We learn little about the possible biases of the sources consulted, such as the interest they may have in exaggerating or minimising levels of crime, or the need to furnish politically acceptable accounts of law enforcement in justifying intervention abroad or hiding collusion at home. Bureaucratic statistics have well-known limitations: such data are produced for internal purposes, often what they say in furnishing the information to those collecting it more centrally will have financial or other implications for them. No study of domestic criminal justice would now rely on official statistics to this extent – so why do so in cross-national work?

Partly because of the sources that they rely on, the textbooks also concentrate overwhelmingly on conventional crime, and it is rare to find much discussion of white-collar and corporate crime, whether local or imported. Crime is assumed to be a problem for everyone, crime control a blessing, under-enforcement and delay a matter of organisational malfunctioning rather than an indicator of political priorities. Little is said about the ways responding to (but not necessarily reducing) local and international crime can serve as a way for governments to gain and maintain legitimacy, or about how criminal justice works to control the poor and ethnic minorities. Terrorism is always *against* the state, never *by* the state (or at least not by 'our' state).

The goals of classification and description predominate over systematic efforts at explanation or interpretation. Classifications of types of jurisdiction borrow heavily from the not always illuminating categories used by comparative law, as with the contrast between the common law and civil law or adversarial and inquisitorial systems. But even reference to more sophisticated efforts to develop classifications can be misleading if account is not taken of social change. Many of the textbooks still rely on Damaška's now classic contrast between common law, 'coordinate', systems and continental, 'policy-oriented', systems (Damaška, 1986) even though we are now living at a time when American 'problem-oriented' courts are a major export (Nolan, 2009). Descriptions of the organisation and functions of police, prosecutors and judges tell us whether they are organised centrally or not. But this is of little help in understanding why, in Italy, for example, the two major national police forces continue to co-exist with overlapping powers – a question that points to the significance of 'redundancy' in the organisation of criminal justice and social control more generally. Little is said about the role of actors other than the police in so-called 'pre-crime' measures of surveillance and crime prevention, as seen in the responsibilities placed on truck drivers and airlines to stop illegal immigration, or the increasing importance of private companies in running prisons.

Differences in various jurisdictions are picked out against the reassuring bedrock of the presumed similarity of 'criminal justice', as if this term is a universal cross-cultural category. Discussions of police, prosecution and courts in the different chapters avoid asking what, if anything, it is that makes them part of a larger 'system'. (The USA, for example, has a highly fragmented federal, state and local system but presupposes its overall coherence. Continental countries have more integrated national systems, but do not always expect or get collaboration between the constituent parts.) Above all, accounts of what goes on in other jurisdictions often pay little or no attention to the differences between the 'law in books' – what the rules say about what is supposed to happen – and the 'law in action' – how the law is or is not used in practice (Pound, 1910; Nelken, 1984, 2009c). Such empirical discussions as are provided give exaggerated 'authority' to dated and controversial empirical forays by English-speaking scholars in the foreign countries concerned. If we are to believe some of the current textbooks, the British are still fighting the IRA. Reliance is placed on a study of juvenile justice in Italy by Edwin Lemert carried out in the 1980s using court data from the 1970s, even though the current system of juvenile procedure has undergone two major changes since then. We are led to believe that such one-off studies can be used somehow to 'represent' the essence of another system of criminal justice – and there is rarely acknowledgement of the differences and internal struggles within each system.

Problems are also created by the disciplinary division in much English-language writing, between those who approach comparative criminal justice from a background in criminology and those who write about it as lawyers interested in criminal procedure. Few of the authors recommending more widespread adoption of common law trial procedures (e.g. Vogler, 2005) address the question of whether this might lead to higher levels of incarceration, even though common law countries are among those with the highest prison rates. In general, little insight is offered about what is involved in making comparisons, the problems of overcoming obstacles of language and culture, and the enormous difficulties that can be faced in trying to understand other ways of life. No real guidance is provided on the actual process of doing cross-cultural research.

Do rates of punishment have anything to do with levels of crime? When (and why) do places punish too much? Why do countries borrow criminal justice innovations from cultures they affect to despise? How can practices be both culturally embedded and yet transferable? How and why do different systems respond as they do to the challenges of transnational crime? Questions such as these cannot easily be addressed within the old descriptive/classificatory paradigm. To get nearer to answers to such matters we need to tackle interpretative problems such as how different societies conceive 'disorder', and how 'differences in social, political and legal culture inform perceptions of crime and the role of criminal agencies in responding to it' (Zedner, 1996).

The choice to cover a lot of ground rather than go into these and other matters certainly reflects the type of student market and the priorities of undergraduate education in a large and varied country such as the USA, where knowledge of even the most basic facts about what goes on elsewhere in the rest of the world cannot be taken for granted. In fairness, too, these authors are often the first to acknowledge the difficulties of finding satisfactory data, and not least, the handicap of working without sufficient studies in depth of the 'law in action' to rely upon. For many of the places being described, it is only recently that relevant empirical material about the 'law in action' has begun to become available. But it can hardly be denied that something of a gulf has grown up between what they present as 'knowledge' and the wider, more varied and ambitious criminological literature that would problematise such 'knowledge'. Moreover, as will be seen in the course of this book, my critique of the field also goes well beyond the textbooks to encompass other scholarly enterprises, including those I describe as 'comparison by juxtaposition', whereby it is assumed, rather than demonstrated, that local experts' accounts of different places are speaking to the same issues, as well as the many studies that place reliance on the commensurability of indicators such as prison rates.

Better answers to why practices of punishment take the form they do in different places have to make reference to the vast historical and social scientific literature available. We need to be able to demonstrate how larger forces shape and are shaped by the details of institutional structures and criminal procedure. We need to pay close attention to the definition and reach of the concepts of crime, of criminal justice and of social control which the observer and the observed employ; the persuasive tropes used in the discourse of criminal justice officials, politicians and criminologists themselves; the changing local and global social contexts which shape what is being studied; the sources of the standpoints being adopted; and the practical purposes and possible implications of research itself. The resources to draw on include, most obviously – but strangely neglected – criminology itself (a 'rendezvous subject' of various disciplines), comparative law, legal theory and philosophy, political economy, political science and sociology, social theory, international law and international relations, and cross-cultural psychology. And this list is far from exhaustive.

Obviously, we should not expect all these disciplines to speak with one voice. For example, history and anthropology in particular, unlike, say, much work in political science or economics, tend to favour interpretation over explanation. Although comparative criminal justice usually borrows from or draws on other disciplines, it may sometimes become a privileged site for challenging them. It may seek to show that the penal state has transformed questions of social inequality, public policy and citizenship (Waquant, 2009a, 2009b), or that comparative criminology may have a better way of estimating the level of killing in Darfur than can be achieved by demographic and health-related approaches (Hagan and Wyland-Richmond, 2008). Finally, even fictional accounts of detective work, trials etc. in books, films and other media may reveal valuable 'truths' about other places, often providing more complex and ambivalent accounts of the motivations and conduct of governments and legal actors than are found in the official sources on which textbooks or other accounts so often choose to rely.

Limits of space in a short book of this kind will not allow me to document all the progress that has already been made towards building the sort of comparative criminal justice being outlined here. But it should be noted that recent contributions increasingly take a broader and more critical approach to the field (e.g. Larsen and Smandych, 2008; Drake, Muncie and Westmorland, 2010a and 2010b). On the other hand, challenging the assumptions of state-centred 'administrative criminology' (Young, 1988) does not in itself provide us with the tools or sensitivities to make sense of rather than impose our own expectations when explaining other peoples' practices – and it is this which is the focus of this book.

The social actors we are studying will not have all the answers to our problems (or their own). But whatever our objectives in studying criminal justice comparatively, we will not get far if we do not do all that is possible to make sure we have a fair grasp of what they think they are doing (as well as what they are actually achieving), and try to find out why it makes sense *to them* – to the extent it actually does so. If, on the other hand, our study of what is thought and happens in other places merely confirms *what we already think is true and right* (the need for more social inclusion, solidarity, tolerance, and respect for difference, for rational policy making and listening to the professionals, etc.), this will often mean that we have projected our ideals and not given sufficient care to analysing all that may lie behind the practices we are studying. The problem is that learning how to avoid this is not easy given that our perceptions of others will always be coloured to some extent by our own cultural starting points.

Policy-makers in the Netherlands, for example, tend to look for pragmatic, practical, workable solutions to crime – just as they do when seeking to resolve other social problems. In Dutch cultural common sense, being pragmatic means *not being dogmatic*. But, in Italy, pragmatic is often taken to suggest behaviour that is not guided by principles, and that therefore borders on being *un*principled. Likewise, the idea of a 'managerial' approach to criminal justice is one that finds little favour, and is widely thought to be something that can potentially interfere with the proper functioning of legal procedures. This is not to say that Italians in everyday life are not often pragmatic, and the Dutch never principled. Far from it. The point is rather that it can be difficult to see the (culturally shaped) limits of a given way of seeing – and to realise, for example, that what we think of as being pragmatic may not actually be that sensible (Brownlie, 1998; Harcourt, 2006). If we insist that pragmatism must have its place, what is its place? If the question is when it is appropriate *not* to be pragmatic, a pragmatic approach may not be able to provide the answer we need.

Outline of book

In seeking to develop these claims further, the following chapters will illustrate their relevance to a number of fundamental issues in comparative criminal justice. Chapter 1 asks why we do comparative research. In Chapter 2 I discuss what is involved in identifying similarities and differences. Chapter 3 examines possible approaches to doing comparative research, concentrating on the differences between explanation and interpretation and the significance of culture. Chapter 4 takes as a case study of explanatory enquiries the debate over differences in prison rates in developed industrial countries. Chapter 5 then addresses the question of how far comparative criminal justice has to change at a time of globalisation. Chapter 6 ends this introduction to the field by providing an account of the role of knowledge itself in the process of comparison. Though these issues are dealt with separately for ease of exposition, an important claim of this book is the need to appreciate how they are related; so there will be frequent cross-references. My aim will be less to take part in the various debates I review than to connect them to my overall theme.

Continuity to the argument will also be provided by the use of examples drawn from the wide range of studies that seeks to contribute to the subject of comparative criminal justice – as well as some that do not. But, in addition, I give special attention to illustrations based on my own empirical research into the workings of criminal justice in Italy, the country whose system I currently know best. As running case studies in each of the chapters, I make reference to three features of criminal justice in Italy that are puzzling, especially to those from an Anglo-American background (see Nelken, 2009b, 2010). The first of these comes from the realm of juvenile justice and has to do with explaining how it is possible that the majority of young Italians charged with murder not only do not go to prison but do not even receive a criminal conviction. What happens to these offenders? Why did this come about and why is nothing done about it? The second has to do with the so-called 'myth of obligatory prosecution', the fact that prosecutors are required – by the constitution itself – to take proceedings in all cases for which there is evidence (if they do not do so, this is itself a violation). Is this principle really respected? How – and how far – is it possible to honour this obligation given the number of cases that are dealt with and the problems of prioritising cases? The final example focuses on the role of delays in Italian courts. What explains why cases take so long – often many years – to go through the various stages and procedures of the trial process? Why has nothing been done about this? Is such a system more or less favourable to the accused than one with effective 'speedy trial' protections?

In using these practices as my illustrations I am not suggesting that they are more important in themselves than the major events that have dominated Italian public life over the last twenty years that have all had, in some way, to do with 'law and order': the series of corruption investigations known as *Tangentopoli*, the vicissitudes of the fight against the mafia and other organised crime groups, the criminalisation of immigrants, or Berlusconi's personal battles with the judges. Certainly, it is only by placing them in context that these practices can be made to seem less strange. But I would insist that giving attention to criminal justice procedures is essential to understanding the shape of such struggles – and sometimes what the struggle is about. And, in terms of comparative enquiry in this field more generally, these case studies allow me to offer a different, and dissenting, perspective on claims about the overall rise of the so-called Penal State that dominate much of the English-language literature.

This said, giving so much attention to Italy, a European, economically developed country with a continental legal system (though one considerably modified as far as criminal justice is concerned) certainly limits the kind of topics in comparative criminal justice I am able to consider. Starting from the experience of the workings of criminal justice in, for example, China, Middle Eastern Islamic countries, or focusing on African forms of dispute resolution, could illuminate different issues – even if it might also obscure others. The textbooks try to cover the larger canvas, and if it could be done well, there would be much to be said for this. But it would be inconsistent with the argument of this book for me to pretend expertise about places that I have never even visited. As I shall argue repeatedly, there is no 'view from nowhere', and no 'global' or 'world view', even if there can be less, or more, parochial perspectives. Hopefully, though, at least some of the theoretical and methodological points that emerge in discussing Italy and the other places touched on may also be applicable in examining criminal justice practices elsewhere.

ONE

why compare?

It may be easy enough to find striking examples of differences in criminal justice, but what is less clear is how these can contribute to make up a coherent subject matter. What is the comparative analysis of criminal justice (good) for? In this chapter I first describe some of the theoretical and policy goals of this subject and how the literature seeks to contribute to them. I then go on to discuss how far this sort of work can overcome the risks of ethnocentrism and relativism.

The goals of comparative criminal justice

There are a variety of theoretical and practical reasons for wanting to know more about what others do about the sanctioning of offensive conduct (Nelken, 1994b, 2002). Whatever misgivings they may have about how their own system works, many people are even more suspicious of what goes on when their fellow citizens end up being tried in courts abroad. Such ethnocentric thinking can easily lead people to assume a priori that their own local arrangements must be superior in general, or at the very least better fitted to their own society. But, fortunately, there are also those who have a more open-minded interest in apparently strange ideas and practices, seeking to make sense of rather than reject difference outright.

Many writers seek to learn from other systems how to improve their own. Hence we get articles with titles like 'English criminal justice: is it better than ours?' (Hughes, 1984), or 'Comparative criminal justice as a guide to American law reform: how the French do it, how can we find out and why should we care?' (Frase, 1990). Those who undertake studies of this kind seek to borrow an institution, practice, technique, idea or slogan so as to better realise their own values, or sometimes to change them. They may aim to learn from those places with high incarceration rates what *not* to do, or they may seek to help others change their systems, for example exporting new police systems to South Africa, or restoring the jury system in Russia. Or again they may just be concerned to cooperate and collaborate in the face of 'common threats'.

But the practical importance of this subject brings us up against one of the most troubling of questions regarding the goals of our comparisons. How far are we intending to learn more about our own system and its problems, and how far are we trying to understand another place, system or practice 'for itself'? For some authors, we can choose between seeking for 'provincial' or 'international' insights, or engaging in 'national' or 'cosmopolitan' enquiries (Reichel, 2008; Zimring, 2006). For reform purposes, comparative researchers deliberately use accounts of practices elsewhere as a foil. Lacey (2008), for example, deploys evidence of differences in prison rates in Europe so as to prove that growing punitiveness is not the only game in town and suggest to UK politicians that they can find a way out of outbidding each other on being 'tough on crime'. In other cases, we may set out to understand the other but end up knowing ourselves. As T.S. Eliot (1943) put it:

> the end of our exploring,
> Will be to arrive where we started,
> And know the place for the first time.

What, on the other hand, could it mean to try to understand another society only in 'its own terms'? Even the society being reported on is likely to *understand itself* in relation to points of similarity and difference in relation to some places (those to which it compares itself) rather than others. To a large extent it is impossible to make sense of things except against some background of previous expectations. Someone from India will find Italian criminal justice relatively efficient; someone from Denmark is unlikely to do so. Any cross-cultural comparison emerges from a given cultural context and has to be able to make sense to the audience(s) for whom it is intended. What is found interesting or puzzling will vary depending on local salience. But even questions couched in terms that *are* salient in both (or more) cultures being compared will lead to different answers depending on which culture one starts from. Reichel (2008) begins his book with the dilemma faced by US police agents, who feel justified to continue to pursue a criminal who has fled to Mexico because the police there are notoriously corrupt. He admits that the Mexican government might feel differently about such conduct. But one would imagine a rather different take on the topic in a textbook written for Mexican students.

Should we then say that what is crucial in studying another place is less whether the author has actually got it 'right' and more what the author makes of it? Balvig, for example (1988), tells us that his aim was less to learn about somewhere else than to understand his own country better. Perhaps this is all that 'learning' from others means (and can mean)? Does it even matter if, according to Johnson (2001), Braithwaite may not have properly grasped the Japanese criminal justice practices he used as a model for his highly influential idea of 'reintegrative shaming' (Braithwaite, 1989)? Taken too far, however, this line of argument becomes self-defeating. The reasons we make comparisons cannot provide the only criterion of success. If we have failed to properly understand another system we can hardly make use of 'it' to throw light on our own arrangements. Even if there is no view from nowhere, this does not prove that all starting points are of equal value. And seeing only what is useful for us is a poor way of acknowledging and engaging with the 'other'.

We also have to ask what, if anything, is specific about this subject. It has been forcefully pointed out that all social science is concerned with explaining variation and difference (Feeley, 1997). Comparison was central to the work of both Durkheim and Weber, albeit with rather different strategies. Many would say that comparison is the essence of all social enquiries or even of logical enquiry in general. In principle, then, no line can or needs to be drawn between criminal justice and comparative criminal justice (or between criminology and comparative criminology). In addition, the traditional focus of what is called comparative criminal justice on different national jurisdictions is mainly a matter of political/legal convention and methodological convenience. There are considerable political, social and cultural differences *within* modern nation-states, for example within the USA (Newburn, 2006), or Australia (Brown, 2005), and even more so in less industrialised societies. For some purposes other 'units', such as towns, organisations and professional groups, can all provide occasions for comparison. And transnational crime activities and responses to them help transform and transcend differences between units defined as nation-states.

The local, the national and the international often interpenetrate. But there may sometimes be good reasons to privilege the nation-state or societal level. States are the locus both for collecting criminal statistics and for administration, and their boundaries often, though not always, coincide with contrasts in language and culture. Franklin Zimring, a distinguished American criminologist, explains that he became a 'convert' to comparative criminology when discovering that Canada had not shared the rise in US prison levels even though its crime rate was not much lower than in the USA, with the exception of homicide and life-threatening robbery (Zimring, 2006). As this example also shows, some of criminology's major debates now involve issues of comparative criminal justice.

Cross-national and cross-cultural research is a fundamental way to show whether criminology's claims are more than local truths (though it does not exhaust this task, in so far as taken-for-granted starting points are also conditioned by other factors, for example gender). But this subject offers a number of other potential benefits (and challenges) that go beyond simply adding to the pool of potential variables that can be used in building criminological explanations. Trying to understand one place in the light of another allows us to move closer to a holistic picture of how crime and its control are connected (what do they know of England who only England know?). For example, it may help us understand the factors that explain why a given society goes through cycles of corruption and anti-corruption. Likewise, it can help us appreciate why reforms that are limited to those that emerge from within the same society often tend to reproduce the problems they are being asked to solve – precisely because they come from the same culture.

In England and Wales, as in the Netherlands, the answer to failures in the system is normally thought to be greater efficiency and speed (as in reforms of the English Youth Justice system inspired by the reports of the Audit Commission). In Italy, a rethinking or defence of 'values' is more often invoked as the way forward when problems arise (thus the 'obligatoriness' of prosecution decision-making is usually argued about as an issue of principle rather than as a question of learning from the 'best practices' of prosecutors as they struggle to deal with this demanding requirement (Nelken and Zanier, 2006)). 'Governing through crime' may be a particularly American obsession, but suggesting that it be replaced with the metaphor of the fight against cancer still remains firmly within the American ethos of instrumental problem-solving (Simon, 2007). Miscarriages of justice arise both in more adversarial and more inquisitorial types of process. But in each case it is their tendency to count too much on the strengths of their procedures that danger lies (Brants, 2010).

Comparative study can help us escape from such self-sealing cultural logics (Field and Nelken, 2007). There are a variety of strategies that can be used. But each is also subject to pitfalls. Classifications can be controversial, descriptions deceptive, explanations erroneous, interpretations interminable, translations twisted, and evaluations ethnocentric. The difficulties multiply in so far as a satisfactory account of difference usually requires the ability to draw on more than one of these strategies. But the message of this book is that considerable progress can be made in understanding and explaining other systems of criminal justice if (but only if) we face up to these challenges.

Collecting data on legal rules, procedures and distinctive institutions is certainly a valuable first step (one that is both demanding and time-consuming, not least because of linguistic and conceptual difficulties). It can be instructive to learn about the social role of policemen in Japan (as well as the lesser known system of voluntary probation officers), or discover that the way chosen to stop traffic policeman in Mexico City taking bribes from motorists was to appoint less threatening women rather than men to do this job. Careful description can also help get beyond often out-of-date classificatory stereotypes. In many respects, the Netherlands has more similarities with the UK than with Italy, even though the UK has a common law rather than continental system of criminal justice. But the task of comparativists, unlike that of lawyers, cannot be that of providing description for description sake. Even the effort to describe selected aspects of criminal procedure in Europe runs to over a thousand pages (Delmas-Marty and Spencer, 2002).

Descriptions can provide the basis for explanation and understanding, but for them to serve this purpose we must have an understanding of the way the 'law in action' relates to the 'law in books'. This essential working tool for all social studies of the law was in fact first put forward in the context of studying police (mis)use of criminal procedure. Likewise, the distance between what continental systems of criminal justice claimed to be doing and what research into the law in action showed they were actually doing was the nub of the classical debate about 'the myth of judicial supervision' in continental criminal procedure (Goldstein and Marcus, 1977). The leading recent empirical in-depth study of French criminal justice, by Jacqueline Hodgson, also places stress on how little actual supervision of police is exercised by continental prosecutors (Hodgson, 2005). On the other hand, if we are worried that some criminal justice systems allow the state to use psychological pressure against defendants (Vogler, 2005), a closer look at what goes on in police cars will quickly show us that this is not a problem restricted to the inquisitorial system.

Empirical research has shown that it was rarely necessary to pass 'telephone justice' messages to judges and prosecutors to ensure politically appropriate outcomes of trials in communist East Germany. The methods used to appoint and socialise recruits to these offices was sufficient (Markovits, 1995). More recently, by contrast, corruption investigations in post-communist Poland were themselves used 'corruptly' against political adversaries under direct government impetus (Polak and Nelken, 2010). As this suggests, rules and safeguards can even operate in ways that are the opposite of what are said to be their justifications. The procedures in Italy that are supposed to protect offenders' rights to know as soon as possible that they are being prosecuted (the *avviso di garanzie* notice) ends up having the effect of facilitating 'trial by media' (Nelken and Maneri, 2000).

Paying attention to the 'law in action' is also relevant to making sense of all three of the running examples being used in this book. The reason why young people in Italy, in some respects, 'get away with murder' is that the 1989 reform of juvenile justice was a procedural one brought in at the same time as the introduction of the major procedural reform in that year for adults. It did not change the substantive penalties on conviction available for serious offences by young people, which remain (in this country where children are so much loved) only prison. The two most important new measures that were introduced – 'irrelevance', for cases that were deemed too trivial for further prosecution (an essential filter in a regime of obligatory prosecution and one not yet available for adults), and 'putting to the test' (*messa alla prova*), a type of probation with in-built requirements of work, schooling etc. – had therefore to be *pre-trial procedures* – ways of putting off and avoiding trial. It is because *messa all prova* is available for all crimes that prosecutions for murder often end up without going to trial provided the conditions of pre-trial probation measures have been successfully met.

Likewise, to make sense of obligatory prosecution, it is necessary to learn how Italian prosecutors actually behave, given the impossibility for handling all the cases on their desk simultaneously. Who or what is it that *de facto* decides priorities – the prosecution office or the single prosecutor – and on what grounds? The rule of obligatory prosecution can in practice strengthen the hands of prosecutors who give priority to some classes of cases rather than others (Nelken, 1997b; Nelken and Zanier, 2006). Finally, to understand the times taken by trials, it is vital to appreciate the workings of the system's own cut-off points for undue procedural delay. This so-called period of *prescription*, within which a case must run its course, applies right up until the hearing of appeal in the final court, after three stages of trial and any number of possible procedural objections. So defence lawyers often try less to prove their client's innocence than to make the case overrun it's allocated time.

For many criminologists, the main interest of comparative criminal justice lies in the help it affords for formulating and testing explanatory hypotheses about levels of incarceration rates, the retention of the death penalty, or whatever. Those looking for explanations of differences in criminal justice practices that translate quickly into policy arguments may be disappointed, however. Asking which penal disposal is better at reducing crime turns out to be more complicated than ever when asked across a range of countries, *many of whose criminal justice systems seem to give low priority to this goal*. We first have to understand why that should be the case. It has been argued that even countries like the USA, which claim to be most concerned with reducing recidivism, are less concerned with crime in its own right than with larger issues of social and moral discipline (Simon, 2007). And critics of penal policies may likewise be as interested in wider questions of how to create a better society as they are in crime rates as such. In this field explanatory and evaluative issues, what works and what is right, are rarely easily separated.

Those with a normative agenda may seek to assess criminal justice systems as a whole. Is the problem that too many people are being sent to prison, or too few, or does all depend on which offenders we are speaking about? There are also interesting differences between criminal justice systems in what kind of evaluation, if any, is seen as appropriate for different actors in the system. Should judges be evaluated, by whom, for what conduct, and for what purpose? (Mohr and Contini, 2008). More commonly, commentators examine what goes on at a given 'stage' of criminal justice, or in one of its constituent organisations or networks. But because criminal justice practices are sites for contesting values, in order to make sense of what criminal justice agents are trying to do, we need to make sense of their normative commitments and will often be providing contestable interpretations of their behaviour.

In Anglo-American systems, for example, it is debatable and debated when plea bargains are to be considered the result of unfair pressures. Getting our normative bearings can be even more difficult in unfamiliar contexts. In Italy, some judges in corruption cases imprison those who refuse to confess, arguing that extracting a confession is the only certain way they have of being sure that the offender will no longer be trusted by his associates (and so be unable to repeat the offence). But many commentators see this as an abuse of criminal procedure. Should 'we' take one side or the other (and who are 'we')? How much allowance should be made for the larger context of political corruption in which judges find themselves, or for particular historical circumstances such as those that characterised the *Tangentopoli* anti-corruption investigations (Nelken, 1996, 1997b)?

Beyond ethnocentrism and relativism?

To make progress both in learning about and evaluating other systems of criminal justice we need to bear in mind two dangers. On the one hand, there is the risk of being ethnocentric – of 'confusing the familiar

Need to understand context

with the necessary'. Here we fall into the trap of assuming that the links between social factors, crime and criminal justice that we find persuasive are also ones that apply generally, and that what *we* do, our way of thinking about and responding to crime, is universally shared, or, at least, that it would be right for everyone else. Alternatively, there is the temptation of relativism. Here the claim is that we can never really grasp what others are doing, or that there can be no transcultural basis for evaluating whether what they, or we, do is right (see, for example, Beirne, 1983/1997; Leavitt, 1990/1997; Cain, 2000b; and Sheptycki and Wardak, 2005).

For some leading post-war authors the point of comparative work was precisely so as to 'uncover etiologic universals operative as causal agents irrespective of cultural differences between different countries' (Szabo, 1975: 367). The search for such generalisations continues. Authors seek to show that certain social groups or categories tend to be more punitive than others, or that similar forms of criminal conduct are, as a matter of fact, universally disapproved to similar degrees. Claims are made that, cross-culturally, people have similar preferences for fair trial processes and shared intuitions about how institutions such as the police must behave if they are to be considered legitimate (Lind and Tyler, 1988). A well-organised criminal justice state that reflects such public preferences is seen as the best way of helping victims of criminal behaviour (Newman, 1999).

The currently renewed interest in establishing and spreading 'evidence-based', transcultural knowledge of 'what works' in responding to crime (Sherman et al., 1997) is an important example of the search for universalistic knowledge in this field. On the one hand, this represents a valuable attempt to reverse the unwarranted, and partially unintended, pessimism induced by the earlier slogan that 'nothing works' in terms of dealing with offenders. But this type of 'globalising criminology' can also be less culture-free than it purports to be (Nelken, 2003a). Strengthening dysfunctional families is seen as the major route to reducing crime. Yet Mafia groups, like those of corrupt politicians and all groups of collaborative criminals, seem, if anything, to suffer from having too strong family or family-like ties. This approach also often gives insufficient attention to what different cultures mean by 'working' (especially in reference to the procedures of criminal justice), as well as for whom it is that crime prevention and criminal justice is supposed to work.

By contrast, there are authors who contest this search for universals and suggest the point of comparative research is rather to undermine the pretensions of positivistic criminology. For them, careful examination of foreign criminal justice practices suggests that it is, above all, the certainties buried in universalising approaches to explanation, such as the claim that all systems find ways of relieving caseload pressures, or that criminal law must always serve the interests of the powerful, that turn out to be cultural rather than scientific truisms. Differences between what societies define and treat as crime can be striking – and not only in the obvious areas of political and sexual deviance. The USA is still sending people to their death in the electric chair, but, in 2008, a fairground owner in Italy was convicted of a crime against public decency for exhibiting a pretend one! The same applies to solutions to deviance. Writers in the UK are convinced that military-style policing always alienates police from the community and so cuts down the supply of information. But in Italy the fact that the militarised *carabinieri* live in barracks apart from society is seen as a guarantee of their independence from potentially corrupting local ties. This is especially important in the South where organised crime groups hold so much sway.

Deciding what is ethnocentric or relativistic is not always straightforward. It is, of course, not ethnocentric to have value preferences – only somewhat suspect if these simply coincide with those we have been brought up to believe in. Thus American textbooks tend to warn of the price that countries such as Saudi Arabia or Japan pay for their low crime or low prison rates. Yes, Saudi Arabia has less crime, but 'we' would not want to have as little 'freedom' as they do. It is true that Japan has low levels of incarceration but some of the things the Japanese do in their criminal process to make this possible we would not find acceptable, and, more generally, 'their 'conformist way of living is not for us (Dammer, Fairchild and Albanese, 2005: 9).

It is moot whether we can use Anglo-American categories, such as 'due process' versus 'crime control' (Packer, 1964), or speak of 'justice' versus 'welfare', as if they referred to universal predicaments. A surprising example of what can be seen as an ethnocentric approach is provided by the great criminologist Edwin Lemert, one of the inventors of the social reaction and labelling approach, and also a specialist in juvenile justice. In a widely reproduced paper about the Italian system, Lemert noted the enormous disproportion between the number of juveniles arrested and processed in the USA and in Italy. But, rather than see this as an indictment of the American approach, he argued that the Italian system was what he called a 'spurious' example of juvenile justice because it could not be seriously considered as trying to implement a welfare system for juveniles on the American model (Lemert, 1986). As it turned out, it was the USA that moved away from the welfare model that the Italian system has been steadily consolidating (Krisberg, 2006).

An emphasis on the importance of diversity and the particular is not the same as relativism (Dembour, 2006). Different arrangements may indeed – rightly – be appropriate under different conditions, and changing conditions may also alter the relevance over time of given values even within the same culture. Roach, for example, argues that the rise of victims' groups challenges the continued utility of Packer's categories, even in Anglo-American settings, by showing that these were focused only on the roles of the state and the accused (Roach, 1998). Even if some practices work well locally, they may not be easily transferable. It is hard to imagine other places copying the Japanese in seeking to reform a rapist by telling him to write a *haiku* (Johnson, 2000). But their wider applicability should not be confused with understanding how they work as they do *in loco*. If the question was how the continental methods of control over the police would work in the USA, then Goldstein and Marcus were right that such methods would be insufficient to avoid potential abuse (Goldstein and Marcus, 1977). But, in so far as the issue was rather trying to understand what other places were actually trying to do, and sometimes succeeding in doing, *in the context of their own structures and expectations*, then Langbein and Weinreb had the better of the argument (Langbein and Weinreb, 1978).

Conversely, if we wish to avoid ethnocentrism, it is not sufficient to be critical of our own practices. This too can be formulated in ways that take for granted local values which are then projected on 'better' systems elsewhere (e.g. Pizzi, 1999). It is often helpful to ask whether we may have fallen into the so-called 'evil causes evil fallacy' (Cohen, 1970). Just as it can be a mistake to assume that the causes of crime must necessarily be other objectionable matters, we need to be open to the possibility that aspects of criminal justice that we disapprove of may be connected to positive and not only negative factors (and vice versa for matters we approve of). Criminologists who try to explain which states in the USA have the highest prison rates tend to single out factors that most criminologists would consider negative in their own right, such as lower welfare levels, less effort to ensure economic equality, and less public participation in political life, or the power of only certain groups to participate where it matters. But this can also be linked to the rise in concern for victims, or the introduction of determinate sentencing through sentencing guidelines. To a limited extent even the effort to abolish or limit the use of the death penalty can increase the use of prison (Gottschalk, 2006). Prison building restarted in the Netherlands in part so as not to abandon the principle of one person to a cell. It has been suggested that egalitarianism in the USA led to an increase rather than a reduction in levels of state punishment (Whitman, 2003; Nelken, 2006e).

More individualist and more collective societies can each have their own sort of pathologies, for example dealing with difference by excluding it or by enforced assimilation (Young, 1999). Assuming that places with lower prison rates necessarily operate more 'inclusive' systems of social justice can be the kind of short-cut that can easily lead to a dead end. Learning from what others do is not so straightforward. On closer acquaintance we may well find that we like the result achieved by other systems of criminal justice, but not the means they use to get there, or vice versa. (In Italy it is the politicians' sense of their vulnerability to criminal prosecution that helps explains why criminal procedure is so complicated, and hence why less people end up in prison than might otherwise do so).

The need to give attention to the local and the particular does not mean that we cannot ever talk about 'best practice', as evaluated according to widely shared standards. Even if considerable caution needs to be used in interpreting cross-national ratings, some places may be doing better or worse in terms of such standards. If one in ten children in Denmark who grow up in local government care homes go on to further education, whereas in the UK only one in a hundred do so, then we would do well to try to learn how this is achieved. But comparative research should not be treated only as a means of identifying universally valid best practices to be adopted wholesale. We can also explore what happens elsewhere so as to engage in 'internal critique' according to our own standards. Those in common law systems could learn that paying more attention to 'due process' considerations could also help achieve the goal of 'crime control' (by increasing legitimacy, public confidence and cooperation). Conversely, French authors could discover that strengthening the role of defence lawyers in their system could help increase the chances of truth emerging from the process – a key value for them.

What this implies is that *the best practice for 'us' to learn from may not always be best practice as such*, but rather that which stretches our imagination about what is possible. Moving a little nearer to what we would otherwise never normally think of doing may be just what is needed. It may seem obvious to many observers of Italy (as well as to some Italians) that the Italian criminal justice system could benefit from increased pragmatism and managerialism. But vice versa, Italy may have something important to teach more pragmatic countries about the possible counter-productive consequences of too much concern for 'efficiency' in their penal systems.

Take the three running examples being used in this book. The Italian juvenile system may seem to offer insufficiently robust procedures for dealing with the type of problem situations that Anglo-American systems face. But, in England and Wales, the government's recent stress on dealing with caseloads more expeditiously mainly led to a substantial rise in youth custody, in contradiction to its general commitment to reduce this number. As far as the rule of obligatory prosecution is concerned, it is not obvious that those who want to bring about a more equal society can or should immediately seek to achieve this by opting for the Italian rule of mandatory prosecution. Even the Italian system achieved the effects it did only during an exceptional period of political transition, though it is also fair to add that the judges themselves played an important part in bringing about that transition. Under 'normal' circumstances, the degree of independence possessed by Italian prosecutors can lead to continual and distracting tests of strength with governments, which weakens collaboration in organising much needed reforms of the criminal process. Nonetheless there may be much to be learned – for countries where prosecution is less independent – about the different possible meanings of prosecutorial independence, and the social and political preconditions and consequences of such independence.

The example of Italian trials raises even more issues. Certainly, justice delayed may often simply be justice denied. Delay reduces the chance of conviction because of its implications for the witnesses' memories, willingness to collaborate, vulnerability to being got at, etc. Once it has accumulated, delay itself produces more delay and uncertainty, and, because final trial verdicts are so slow in coming, Italy is increasingly experiencing trial by media as the daily newspapers treat even information about the earliest stage of an investigation as a token of presumed guilt. But, in so far as delay is produced by given rules of criminal procedure, this should lead us to think more carefully what 'due process' (what the Italians call *garanzie*) should actually require. How many stages of appeal should there be? How much need is there for separate scrutiny at each stage by different judges (and how appropriate is it to restrict all such decisions to legally trained people)? Why is it not enough to trust to the system's own internal legal definition of when cases have overrun the time in which they must be disposed of?

We can even ask whether slowness can ever have value. At a conference in Padua on the topic of legal delay in which I participated, it was surmised that delayed trials could give victims time to get over their upset so as not be so emotional. This may seem less strange a suggestion if we treat criminal justice, as one important progressive Italian theorist does, as primarily a means to restrain vendetta in the interest of the offender (Ferrajoli, 1989; Nelken 1993). This is certainly a very different perspective from the current trend to make the victim and his and her feelings play a more central role. Criminal justice also reflects wider social values. A more efficient or speedy court system in Italy would often come into conflict with a social structure and culture in which many people place reliance on slowly built-up forms of group co-optation and clientalist sponsorship, sometimes even in defiance of legal rules. On a more positive note, Italy has been called the spiritual home of the slowness movement, the call to all of us to slow down so as to get more out of life (Honoré, 2004). Perhaps slow food and fast trials are incompatible?

TWO

just comparison

What makes for a fair comparison? Where do and should we start from in making comparisons? Should we be looking for similarities or for differences? What do we mean by comparing like with like? The answer to these questions depends in large part on the point of the exercise, on what is being compared, and on why. Hence the discussion in this chapter is connected to all the others in this book. The main point I seek to make here, however, is that difficulties in finding answers to these questions should be seen less as practical obstacles to be got over or got round and more as clues to understanding difference.

Starting points

Where we begin is all-important in any comparison. It is too easy just to fasten on differences in national statistics about criminal justice and then seek to explain them. Too often, however, this means we presuppose rather than learn how to change our intellectual coordinates. To do this we need to seek out puzzles and then make sense of them. But enigmas do not exist in the abstract; they emerge when relating what is considered salient in the place concerned – its own starting points in thinking about crime and criminal justice – to what is salient for the investigator. Once, when I remarked impatiently that a particularly convoluted bureaucratic requirement in Italy was 'Kafka-like', a colleague replied sharply 'It's Kafka to you!' (But perhaps that is also what the good citizens of Prague may have said to Kafka?).

There certainly are criminal justice practices that can be considered strange even in supposedly more pragmatic cultures. What sense is there in allowing, as the Dutch do, the retail sale of marihuana to customers in 'coffee-houses' while continuing to prohibit the wholesale supply of it to the same places at the back door? How would Americans explain to foreign observers that one Reagan appointee to the Federal Office of Juvenile Justice and Delinquency Prevention carried a bumper sticker on his car reading 'Have you slugged your kid today' (Krisberg, 2006: 8). The UK government allows shopping malls to deter unwanted bands of young people by using 'mosquito' machines that emit annoying sounds that can only be heard by youngsters; the not always as effective alternative, apparently, being to play popular music records from the 1950s (Crawford, 2010). That these last two examples both have to do with young people is not happenstance.

The point is that unless we can somehow get a grasp on the ways our cultural assumptions shape our comparative projects we are unlikely to make progress in understanding another society. For example, as compared to socio-economic factors, the role of religion and the family currently finds little space in many cross-national explanations of prison rates. But this may have mainly to do with the socio-cultural starting point of those doing the comparing. What are considered problems and solutions varies from place to place, and from time to time. Zedner reports that she had difficulty in convincing colleagues at Chicago during a visit there that gun-carrying by teenagers was not in fact the pre-eminent problem of crime-control everywhere (Zedner, 2003: 167). If we keep reading about corruption in Italy and less so in the UK (at least until recently) this could be not only because there actually is more corruption in Italy but also because it is more salient there (Eve, 1996). Starting points also shape what are seen as appropriate solutions. To a large extent, in Anglo-American countries (as Continental Europeans refer to them) a solution is widely considered right because it 'works'. But, in the less policy-dominated discourse in Italy and some other continental countries, it would be as true to say that, for many commentators, a response 'works' because it is 'right', and less attention is given to what actually happens as opposed to what ought to happen.

In Italy, until recently, it was common for the victim (or relatives of victims) of horrendous crimes to be asked by journalists if they were willing to forgive the offender (rather than being enlisted by politicians or journalists so as to show the need for greater severity). But things change. For one leading author writing about Italy in the 1990s, the concern was less about 'governing through crime' (Simon, 2007) than 'ruling through leniency' (Melossi, 1994), as shown in the willingness of governments to rule without contesting the power of organised crime groups. But, even in Italy, campaigns against crime by immigrants have become an excuse for giving more attention to 'victims' (usually ignoring the relatively high proportion of immigrants who end up as victims of serious crimes). Melossi himself now focuses his work less on leniency than on the serious problem of the criminalisation of immigrants. If Zedner's colleagues from Chicago had visited London in the summer of 2008 they would have found considerable concern over deaths caused by knife-carrying youngsters.

These points about structures of relevance have important implications for projects involving collaboration between experts in a various countries. Sometimes the hope is that important cross-national similarities and differences will emerge from detailed descriptions of what goes on in different places. Michael Tonry, for instance, assembled leading scholars to describe what was happening to crime and punishment in their respective countries (Tonry, 2007b). Junger-Tas and Decker (2006) collected reports from a large range of experts more specifically on developments in juvenile justice. At other times editors explicitly invite their contributors to address a common issue. Thus Pratt et al. (2005) and Muncie and Goldson (2006) ask their contributors to focus on the issue of where the countries and systems they are describing stand on the issue of growing punitiveness. Alternatively, a more elaborated hypothesis may be put forward for testing cross-nationally. In their study of police integrity, Klockars, Ivkovich and Haberfeld (2004) standardised a survey instrument to be administered to police organisations in a variety of countries. This was intended to measure the extent to which reported expectations about possible internal sanctions likely to be forthcoming from the organisation were correlated with reports of the frequency of inappropriate behaviour actually taking place.

There is much to be learned from these books. But, while the chapters are often of high value in their own right as guides to local developments, what emerges is often only of tangential relevance to cross-national generalisations. Junger-Tas and Decker's main finding, for example, says little more than that there are consistent differences between what has been happening in Anglo-American and Continental European jurisdictions. Contributors to these types of collective work are themselves often caught in a dilemma of how far to tell us all about their own country in terms of local concerns and how far to follow the editor's guidelines and refer to the common trend or hypothesis. The best way to explain what is happening locally may be neither in terms of the system following a common trend nor in terms of it resisting it (see e.g. Nelken, 2005).

As far as testing hypotheses is concerned, it is not easy to move between the general and the particular. Klockars, Ivkovich and Haberfeld were searching mainly for cross-national and cross-cultural explanatory 'universals' about the relationship between organisational culture, police misbehaviour and the responses to it. They claimed to show that police officers in general agreed about the relative seriousness of forms of police misconduct, but their survey instrument was particularly apt for the decentralised USA, where different police agencies vary enormously in how far they tolerate police misconduct. However, the authors of the Swedish contribution paid little attention to local variation, and much more to that between the sexes. For them, the problem of public police running private security businesses had a symbolic importance that was not necessarily generalisable. More radical still, the survey of Japanese police showed an impressive level of integrity. But the author cautioned that this could be due to the cultural norms that oblige the police in Japan to reply to enquiries in certain ways, and suggested that the real problems of police integrity lay at the top, in particular in police collusion with gambling and organised crime.

The question of salience is also linked to the units that we do or should use as the reference points of our comparisons. The assumption is that some places are more important than others for the contribution they can provide in clarifying issues in comparative criminal justice. Many textbooks talk, for example, about model nations, prototypes, archetypes, etc. (Pakes, 2004; Dammer, Fairchild and Albanese, 2005).

But the choice of which nations to discuss seems somewhat haphazard. Some places, such as Japan, Switzerland and Saudi Arabia, have lent themselves to be used as exemplars of large possible differences in crime rates or prison rates. Among Western industrialised countries the USA is, in some respects, the most exceptional country (not only for the size of its prison population, but also in the centrality of criminal justice as a form of social control). But, given that it is the place where most textbooks are written, much writing about criminal justice assumes it as a background, and its approaches often spread by imitation elsewhere. By contrast, some other countries, such as the allegedly more 'inclusive' and tolerant Scandinavia countries, are currently idealised because of their relatively low incarceration rates. But such places are much more complicated when taken in their own terms and not only treated as exemplars of leniency. Thus Finland is strongly committed to repress drug dealing, and Sweden to cutting down prostitution.

The units of comparison to which scholars refer tend, mainly for reasons of convenience, to be nation-states, although categories taken from comparative law are also common. More imaginative comparisons use units which reflect differences in religious affiliation, between 'guilt' and 'shame' societies, or ideas about 'high-context' and 'low-context' cultures, and so on. In addition to comparing states or societies, some authors compare sub-units, subcultures, organisations and even actors within criminal justice systems. So-called 'epistemic communities' (Karstedt, 2002) of regulators or scholars also represent possible units for comparison.

It is not always clear when we should favour multi-sited research as compared to single case studies. (Even studying a single society counts as a comparative study if it is being conducted as an implicit comparison with one or more other societies.) Zimring distinguishes between what he calls 'distributional' and 'contextual' comparative work (Zimring, 2006). To see variations across places, he claims, is useful if we are dealing with Italy, but essential if we are studying Belgium. On the other hand, a focus just on the USA, he argues, can be justified so as to isolate what is special about it. But we could also say that, depending on our purposes, even smaller jurisdictions could sometimes need to be studied contextually. What is clear is that the larger the number of societies being compared, the more difficult it will be to formulate variables that are salient cross-culturally. On the other hand when only a limited number of places are compared, it is possible to be misled by missing the larger picture. Some early comparisons between the American and Japanese criminal justice systems left out of consideration the fact that it was European Continental models that shaped legal institutions in Japan – something which would have done much to explain features which to American eyes were taken to be characteristically Japanese. The much lower incarceration rate in Italy as compared to the USA is less interesting once Italian rates are seen to be in line with those in Europe more generally. Indeed, it ceases to be something that tells you much about Italy as such.

Depending on our purposes a large variety of 'units' may be usefully compared. We can compare whole societies, as in identifying distinct patterns to European and American ways of responding to threats like drug trafficking (Fukumi, 2009), or nation-specific approaches to stopping human trafficking (Munro, 2006). Or we may seek to sharpen our understanding of different features within criminal justice systems, whether they be police practices, prosecution procedures, the rights of victims and defendants, negotiated justice, or the influence of the media (Delmas-Marty and Spencer, 2002). We may thus discover that the antibodies to political corruption in Europe are (or were) mainly to be found in the bureaucracy in Germany, in the judiciary in Italy, and in Parliament in the UK (Della Porta and Meny, 1997).

Just as many comparisons in criminology consider the influence of general trends, such as the growing period before young people find work or increasing immigration, so the same applies to developments in dealing with crime problems. We can look for differences across places in the rise of preventative measures or restitutive justice, the decline in the power of the state as compared to the market, or the loss of faith in some professions accompanied by the rise of new ones. But working out the various implications of trends can be complicated. There may, for example, be growing intolerance of some kinds of behaviour but increasing tolerance of others. Hence, in addition to examining differences in criminal justice systems seen statically, we must also investigate their dynamics as they each react differentially to similar kinds of challenge over time. Litigation or administrative remedies may offer two contrasting, though not necessarily equally effective, routes to protecting prisoners' rights, but the balance between them may change

(Lazarus, 2004). Often a _cause célèbre_ provides a good opportunity for comparative analysis. Consider, for example, the different responses in the UK and Norway to extreme cases of murder by young children (Green, 2007). Interestingly, the Italian juvenile justice system, despite allowing most juveniles accused of murder to be dealt with by pre-trial probation, drew the line in the so-called Erica and Omar case, where a pair of middle-class teenagers killed the girl's mother and younger brother. Their lawyer did in fact ask for this disposal, but they actually received 16 and 14 years in prison.

On similarities and differences

All comparison involves the identification of similarities and differences over space and time. Why do nation-state prison rates tend to group together at the same level by geographical areas? (Aebi and Stadnic, 2007). If Italy and Spain share many similarities in their criminal justice systems (including their current criminalisation of immigrants), how much this is to do with their political economies and how much to do with their histories and religious traditions? Or comparative work can involve arguing that what seems different is really similar, and vice versa. Showing similarities or difference in itself, however, is not enough. We must have theoretical justifications for showing why our findings are interesting (because unexpected). It is usually of limited interest to demonstrate that societies do not behave as would be expected according to ideal-type classifications of families of law. Such discrepancies may only tell us about the weakness of our starting points.

If the issue is how to look for the unexpected, it may be helpful to bear a number of rules of thumb in mind. First, we need to avoid assuming similarity at all costs. As Geertz puts it, 'the comparative study of law cannot be a matter of reducing concrete differences to abstract commonalities ... law is local knowledge not placeless principle' (Geertz, 1973: 215). Indeed, some leading comparative sociologists have insisted that at a time where forces conducing to homogenisation are so strong, we should focus more on differences than similarities. The particular is not only often more interesting than the general; politically speaking, it is the right choice, because we should be seeking to preserve particularity and diversity (Sztompka, 1990). Sexual offences and corruption are particularly rich areas for cross-cultural comparison. In Japan, President Clinton's wife would have had to apologise for her husband's conduct (West, 2009). Such differences remind us of the need to descend from the high level of abstraction, where it is too easy to assume that there must be more similarities than differences.

On the other hand, we also need to be aware that differences can be and often are exaggerated (although the 'social achievement' of constructing such purported differences may in fact be what we want to explain). It has been plausibly claimed by a leading author that Continental Europe is more receptive to rationalistic technology transfers whereas England and the USA are more resistant to abstract ideas (Tonry, 2001). But the idea of rights is crucial in the USA and even the UK played an important role early on in drafting the UN Declaration of Human Rights. Thus, although I have given this book the subtitle *Making Sense of Difference*, sometimes the challenge may be more to explain similarities than differences (in so far as they are different from what we would expect). *Comparative work is both about discovering surprising differences and unexpected similarities.* Setting out to demonstrate that all higher courts play a central and less than independent role in ensuring governmental social control becomes a provocative argument if the cultures surveyed are as different as Muslim, Chinese, French and British (Shapiro, 1981). We may want to explain why judicial power is growing in places otherwise as different as Italy and Thailand.

The search for differences is often motivated by the desire to show the limits of supposedly universal claims (though without necessarily assuming a priori the impossibility of finding cross-cultural truths and values). Johnson's work on prosecutors in Japan was intended not only to show their lack of interest in producing convictions, but also to criticise those (largely US) scholars who argued that 'all prosecutors', by the nature of their job, aim to maximise convictions (Johnson, 2000). Italy, too, can provide valuable examples for this purpose. Criminal justice usually targets the poor and less powerful and offers immunity to the more powerful. Yet in the 1990s the judges managed to use the criminal law there so as to cancel all the traditional parties of government (Nelken, 1996).

One clue to interesting similarities and differences can be found in 'significant absences', as Lacey and Zedner argue when describing and explaining the historical reasons for the absence of a discourse about 'community justice' in Germany (Lacey and Zedner, 1998). In Italy, why are policemen rarely seen as authoritative spokesmen on the crime problem? Why do popular newspapers there still have less power to shape political action over crime than in the USA and the UK? Understanding the causes, consequences and meaning of such 'significant' differences in fact requires interpretation and explanation of both *absence* and *presence* in each of the cultures concerned. To understand the role played by laymen in criminal justice in Britain as opposed to Italy, it would be necessary to investigate *both* the reasons why the involvement of laymen is favoured in Britain as well as what state officials symbolise in Italy. If the Italian system of criminal justice has relatively more built-in leniency than the Anglo-American system, we need to explain both the comparative indulgence of the first and the harshness of the other.

Working out the significance of absence and presence can be even more complicated than this. *Absence has a shape*, in the sense that there may be a definite sense of what is missing. Many Italians bemoan the lack of a well-functioning state, and though they mainly lambast their politicians, they also sometimes blame themselves (the expression 'we don't have the sense of the state' is heard frequently). But the state they feel the absence of is quite definitely the French or German idea of the state, with its collective project taken forward by the organs and officials of the nation, rather than the 'foreign' English or American liberal conception of government as the servant of civil society (Dyson, 1980). In the European tradition 'the legal system is the way the state makes ethical the system of needs of civil society' (Melossi, 1990: 100–2). From this continental perspective it is the Anglo-American ideas of the state, one in which popular sovereignty replaced the role of the ideal representative of social and political stability, and in which private interests have an inherent legitimacy, which seemed, and can still seem, strange (Ferrarese, 1997).

When it comes to identifying distinctiveness on the basis of 'absence and presence', we need to be aware that legal and political discourses may have only an uncertain relationship to social practices. The observer may find the 'problem' or threat to be similar, but the rhetoric very different – or vice versa. Both practice and discourse therefore need to be studied independently as well as in relation to each other. In one country, the debate may centre on public order policing, while, in practice, police surveillance goes on unnoticed; another culture may be concerned about the risks of private surveillance, but take for granted the role of public police patrols (Zedner, 1995: 526–7). The relationship between discourse and practice can also be paradoxical. The Italian national state is, *in theory*, a collective impersonal project. *In practice*, however, its survival with any sort of credibility often comes down to the calibre and integrity (or the lack of these qualities) of a very limited number of individual politicians, judges or policemen, some of whom risk martyrdom in its name. In Britain there is much less use of the notion of 'the state' as compared to simply talking in a relatively personalised way about the government of the day. But there seems to be no contradiction at all between this talk of individuals and strong identification with the nation-state (helped by, but surely not reducible to, the institution of the monarchy).

Comparing like with like

It is commonly said that a comparison is only valid if we are comparing 'like with like', but teasing out what this means is not easy. As Sztompka (1990: 47) asks: 'What makes a difference a difference? When is the same really the same, when is the same really different?' For some purposes, it can even be useful to compare like with unlike, as when Hagan looks for similarities in 'exclusion' in the global north and global south (Hagan and Wyland-Richmond, 2008). Could the way the UK deals with white-collar criminals have at least something interesting in common with the methods Italy uses for handling juvenile delinquents in the way it seeks to avoid criminalisation at all costs? What some see as the 'narcissism of small differences', others may regard as very important, as when scholars insist on the differences in the USA and English versions of 'zero tolerance', or point to considerable differences in the way common law countries interpret the role of problem-solving courts (Nolan, 2009). Continental Europeans often talk of the Anglo-American type of law, but common law scholars point to profound differences between the formalism of the English system of law as compared to the substantive approach of American law.

Considerable argument and evidence may be needed to show whether or not extraneous matters undermine the point of a comparison. On the one hand, what is being compared will always be different in some respect or else there would be nothing to compare. On the other hand, unappreciated differences in respect of relevant features of what we are trying to understand can be so significant as to undermine the value of any given comparison. Can juvenile justice in Italy be properly compared with that in the UK, given the larger role of the family in Italy? Is that the key to the comparison or rather a factor that takes away its point? When Savelsberg and King (2005) point out how much more Germany has institutionalised efforts to seek public atonement for the Holocaust/Shoa than American governments have done for their genocide of Native Americans (or for the victims of slavery and the slave trade), there may be some who think it debatable whether this is comparing like with like. But it is a debate worth having.

What is meant by comparing 'like with like' is the effort to hold constant in our comparison those factors – regarding time frames, threats, legal systems, economies, politics or whatever – which would otherwise take away the point of a given comparison. At the same time, however, it is usually reference to those factors that will also form part of our explanation of difference. It is the apt choice of constants which set up the puzzle at the heart of any worthwhile comparison: the more the constants would seem to cover relevant factors, the more surprising and instructive the finding of difference. Why do different countries in the European Union deal with similar European Union frauds so differently? (Passas and Nelken, 1993). If victims have the 'same needs' in Germany and the UK, why is the police response and the activity of victim groups so different? Why are victims even more satisfied in Germany despite getting less attention than they do in the UK? (Mawby and Kirchoff, 1996). Why, under the same type of communist system was the role of prosecutors weak in Poland but strong in Russia? And why does that still remain true? (Polak and Nelken, 2010).

The central claim of this book is that we will face difficulties in identifying what to hold constant unless we already know quite a lot about the places being compared (and the larger the number of units being compared the more tricky this can be). To compare levels of punitiveness it is not enough just to compare prison rates. We can and must go beyond mere quantitative measures of penal sanctions so as to add a qualitative dimension of 'harshness', for example with respect to the way prisoners are treated (Whitman, 2003). But even this may not be enough to be sure we are comparing like with like. What should we do about other types of social control that exist in a given society? What of the fact that, in some countries, the numbers held involuntarily in other types of total institution, especially mental asylums, have fallen almost in proportion to the rise of the numbers in prison? Even if there is no simple transfer of populations going on here, we should not lose sight of this reverse trend to decarceration. A generation back the fear was that the proliferation of such 'soft' social control would lead to the growth of the 'punitive city' (Cohen, 1985). Are we now just to ignore such types of punitiveness? Current 'penal technologies' bundle together risk prevention and welfare strategies for different offences and offenders in ways that undifferentiated talk of punitiveness fails to capture.

If the number of black people imprisoned in the USA rose seven times in the later nineteenth century after the abolition of slavery, this surely must have implications for measuring the level of punitiveness before and after that event. Limiting our discussion only to changes in prison rates would certainly be misleading. But, if this is true in looking at US prison rates over time, we can imagine at least as great difficulties when we engage in cross-cultural comparisons. What of the fact that the police in Pakistan, Brazil and elsewhere are said to be involved in thousands of semi-institutionalised killings yearly? (Johnson and Zimring, 2008). Both the Mafia in Italy and the *Yakuza* organised crime groups in Japan are involved in social control (with, at the extreme, their own form of death penalty). Why should this not count when considering the statistics of penal control?

Some American textbooks do bring in so-called 'informal' social control as the explanation of differences in criminal justice in discussing low prison rates in Japan and Saudi Arabia. Japan may have comparatively few people in prison, but the risks of ostracism for rule-breaking may often be considerable. Sociologists of the family in Italy speak of a generation living in a 'gilded prison' that has had little chance to have any political role in society. But it is not simply that other forms of social control supplement official criminal justice. Criminal justice itself may be understood primarily as the control of the poor (Waquant, 2009a, 2009b), or a way of reinforcing the restrictions on racial or ethnic groups (Tonry, 1995), though how (far) this is true will vary from place to place.

In addition, and contrary to the claims of some behavioural sociologists of law (Black, 1976), there is no reason to assume that repressiveness in the wider society ('informal social control') and the use of prison ('governmental social control') are inversely correlated. We can, for example, identify societies, such as China, that are both repressive and have high prison rates, and others that are repressive but have low prison rates, such as present-day Saudi Arabia, or Spain under Franco. Where the USA, with its high prison levels, fits into this picture is more uncertain. Certainly, law enters in detail into every part of life – and criminal law since 9/11 and the Patriot Act has been ever more ubiquitous. Simon's celebrated analysis of 'governing through crime' (Simon, 2007) argues that the metaphors and methods of criminal justice have been replacing other forms of social control in the family, the school and the workplace. But relative to many other places, the USA still, in some respects, bestows an unusual level of political and religious freedoms on groups and individuals.

The fact that we are always holding some things constant means that we are rarely dealing only with similarities or differences. Rather, what we will usually need to explain is the *unfamiliar mixture* of both in any given case. Noting this can help us avoid the common error of seeing patterns of criminal justice elsewhere as made up of only their differences – and not also by their similarities to us. Cities in the USA and Europe are governed differently but social control is built into urban design in both places (Body-Genrot, 2000). Surveillance in Japan has similarities with that found in Western countries, but it also has suggestive specificities (Wood, 2009).

When we set out to 'tell difference' (Nelken, 2000b) we always need to think 'as compared to what?' It would not be difficult to point to much that is special about crime and criminal justice in Italy: the level of organised crime (with four powerful crime groups conditioning political and economic life in much of the south), the unresolved problem of political corruption, the struggle between the long-standing Italian premier Berlusconi and the judges he regularly accuses of persecuting him, the delays that afflict the legal system, and so on.

But there are also many similarities in how criminal justice works in Italy and advanced Western societies, and the commonalities between Italian and many other Continental European approaches are even greater. We can find parallels in Italy to many of the developments and concerns that are at the centre of research on criminal justice in Britain and other English-speaking countries. In both settings there is considerable discussion of the exponential increase in crime since the Second World War and the more recent apparent growth in the fear of crime. The same types of socially and economically marginal people fill up the prisons, usually for offences involving theft or drug dealing. Likewise, the evolution of crime prevention follows much the same pattern and local government initiatives are taking on some of the responsibilities previously monopolised by the state. Along with increasing resort to technology, such as investment in closed-circuit television, there is a massive growth in private policing in securing the safety of banks, and the 'public-private' spaces of shopping malls, though not as yet so much as an essential part of housing developments for the rich.

In Italy, too, we can discover experiments in mediation between offenders and victims, especially in cases involving juveniles. It also takes part in international victim surveys and organises annual victim surveys for internal monitoring of its crime problem. Slogans such as 'zero tolerance' are used by political campaigners of different persuasions, both by the mayor of Milan responding to social alarm over increased street crime, and by women's groups taking forward their struggle against assault and harassment in the home and at work. All over the world, Italy included, public opinion about crime is increasingly shaped by the 'virtual' knowledge produced by the media and this in turn shapes police action as they seek to build legitimacy and defend their resources.

To some extent it is a matter of choice whether to emphasise similarities or differences, and this choice will often depend on the purposes of our comparisons. We may be tempted to argue that we cannot learn from practices in another society because it is 'too different' from ours.

But sometimes an institution is borrowed in the hope it will actually help make the borrowing society more similar! Claims about both similarities and differences, or normality and exceptionality, can have consequences and be exploited for political purposes. The elites in post-war Finland sought to bring down their incarceration rates so as to be more in line with other Scandinavian countries. The Canadians keep a watchful eye on their own rates so as to show how very much lower they are than those in their powerful neighbour but seem less concerned that their rate is higher than those in Europe. Policy-makers in Scotland would like to think that their criminal justice system is more enlightened than that of England and Wales – and sometimes it is.

Societies, institutions, places, rates, ideas can all be exceptional or 'normal'. But findings about the existence of difference or similarity are not in themselves 'progressive' or otherwise. This depends on the specific arguments advanced. As Maureen Cain has argued, we need to take care that our comparisons do not fall into the vices of either Occidentalism or Orientalism, i.e. making other cultures seem necessarily similar to ours, or intrinsically 'other' (Cain, 2000b). *Pace* Sztompka (1990), too much insistence on difference can also sometimes be a form of 'othering'. There is no denying that external influences often produce pressure for change to 'normality', but sometimes they also come from within. A variety of Italian writers, just after the *Tangentopoli* investigations had revealed widespread political corruption, wrote books bemoaning the fact that Italy was not a 'normal' country. On the other hand, 'best practice', by definition, is also not normal.

THREE

ways of making sense

The theoretical approaches we draw on to develop persuasive accounts of the workings of criminal justice in different places will vary according to the topics being investigated. As is seen in some of the most powerful recent analyses, such as those of Garland (2001) or Waquant (2009a, 2009b), we need to draw on both the materialist and symbolic dimensions of punishment. In line with the major theme of this book, I limit myself here to discussing the basic question of how we attribute or grasp meaning. First, I contrast explanatory and interpretative enquiries and say something about how such strategies can be brought together. I then go on to consider how the choice of approach shapes the place of terms like 'culture' and 'legal culture' in our attempts to make sense of difference.

Explanation versus interpretation

The choice between causal explanation and empathetic interpretation, or between nomothetic and idiographic approaches to social behaviour, are vexed and still controversial questions within the methodology and history of the social sciences. On one approach, still dominant in the influential USA criminological literature, our task is to search for cross-culturally valid explanations. The role of science is to get beyond common sense and the individuals we are studying may not know the causes and consequences of their actions (especially the unintended ones which are often the result of unexpected combinations with others). In categorising countries or societies as more or less religious (for example, in relation to the retention of the death penalty) we do not necessarily need to approach this causal factor as participants themselves would understand it. The choice of which variables to study will be based on previous research by the community of scholars; each new research then seeks to take matters further.

By contrast, for more interpretative approaches, intentional social action is what produces social outcomes. Religion as a key factor effecting outcomes must therefore be religious teaching as understood by those involved. This can help us understand why links between religion and aspects of criminal justice can be different in different places and at different times. Social actors can draw selectively on their cultural heritages as a 'tool-kit' or resource (Melossi, 2001). For classical writers, such as Weber our accounts must be persuasive both at the level of cause and the level of meaning. But there are even those who would reject any search for causes and move enquiry more into the realm of 'how' than that of 'why' questions. They would focus on the shared construction of meaning – on how and when the efficacy of 'religion' is invoked, and by whom.

There are leading writers in this field of social research, just as in others, who line up more towards one or other end of this continuum. On the one hand, we could take Greenberg and West (2008) as a model example of a cross-national study of variables carefully correlated with the use of the death penalty (that shows religion to be the decisive determining factor). At the other extreme, in his subtle account of policy-making for victims of crime in Canada, Paul Rock tells us that developments cannot be analysed with 'clear cause and effects' since events 'fold back on each other' and 'officials make causes through their arguments rather than vice versa' (Rock, 1986: 67ff). But it would be a pity if comparative criminal justice were to become just a battle-ground for proponents of different approaches to explanation (Travers, 2008). To stress the value of interpretation in cross-cultural enquiries does not imply, as some argue, a commitment to relativism (Pakes, 2004: 13), or make it impossible to establish 'non-contextual truths' (Edwards and Hughes, 2005). There is nothing relativist about the claim that the correlations we investigate or discover become 'explanations' only when given 'sense' by theoretical hypotheses shaped by our different cultural experiences (which accounts for why we find some explanations more 'plausible' and normatively attractive than others). Rather than claiming that interpretative understanding should replace the search for explanation, I have insisted on the need to combine these two approaches (Nelken, 1994b), arguing that 'understanding' must come 'before', as well as 'after', 'explanation' (Nelken, 2002). Urging comparativists to be more reflexive about which variables they select for their explanations is a goal that only a non-relativist would bother to pursue.

The choice between explanation and interpretation often also overlaps with – even if it should not be confused with – the difference between quantitative and qualitative approaches and macro-social and micro-social levels of analysis. Large-scale quantitative cross-cultural comparisons in particular require some sort of common denominator of meaning for key dependent variables such as rates of crime and punishment. But these cross-national penal 'indicators' can often obscure what needs to be understood. Take, from among the wealth of tables classifying different aspects of criminal justice to be found in Van Dijk's recent comprehensive sourcebook, the one that has to do with judicial independence. We are told that Italy's judiciary comes rather low down on the criterion of 'independence'. The judges in the UK, by contrast, are among the very highest (Van Dijk, 2007: 376; the UK gets a score of 6, the USA 5.7, Italy only 4.4.).

Perhaps this is so. But a lot depends on what is taken to be 'independence'. Independence from whom? (The government? The public?) This indicator is in fact built out of the perceptions of businessmen as to which judiciaries are most independent of undue pressure of government, private persons or firms. But theirs is not the only relevant perspective, especially when it comes to issues of criminal justice. In Italy, for much of the past twenty years, following its anti-corruption successes, the judiciary has been under constant attack by politicians, who see it as having far *too much* independence (Nelken, 1996). As in most places on the continent, judges are neither appointed nor elected, but selected by public examination immediately after university. They therefore represent a wide range of the political spectrum. In addition, in Italy, prosecutors are considered part of the judiciary and are, like them, constitutionally immovable from their posts. Their promotion and pay is almost entirely tied only to seniority (even without the need of changing job) and not to the dictates of politicians who, it is feared, might otherwise exercise a conditioning effect on their decision-making. Decisions over who gets senior administrative roles, internal discipline and so on are made by the judiciary's own elected parliament, which protects what they call their 'autonomy' from government.

By contrast, until recently, judges in England were appointed by the government from successful middle-aged lawyers – on the advice of a senior judge who is also a minister. Sensitive prosecution decisions are in the hands of another government minister, and in a number of recent cases there have been real doubts about how far government interpretations of the national interest have been placed above the normal rules of criminal law. Turning to the USA, many judges are elected by the citizenry, while, for those who are appointed, the ability to curry political favour and mix with the local elites is an essential part of the job. Of course there is always more that can be said. There are documented cases of some Italian judges who have been found to be corrupt, and it is a moot question whether the allegiance that many judges in Italy have to the quasi-political groupings that elect their representatives in the judges' parliament weakens their independence as single judges. Is the low score intended as a measure of the political attacks to which judges are exposed? But resistance to these attacks might equally be seen as proof of how independent they are.

Interpretative types of enquiry, on the other hand, are the preferred option where the aim is to show congruence between meanings and values in criminal justice and the larger culture. For example, how ideas about the state and citizen are reflected and reproduced by the role assigned to the accused in French criminal justice (Field, 2006). They are also essential when we set out to make sense of puzzling events. How can it be, asked a well-informed American commentator on Italian affairs in 2008, that on the very day that Prime Minister Berlusconi's English lawyer was convicted in an Italian court of lying to protect the prime minister, it was the leader of the Italian opposition who resigned. As Becker reminds us, the first rule when we are faced with a strange social phenomenon should be to assume that there is some sense to be found if we can only find a way to grasp it (Becker, 1997: 28).

There are important differences between explanatory and interpretative approaches. We risk inconsistency if we insist on the 'embeddedness' of meaning but also try to use 'objectified' prison rates as part of our explanations of different penal climates (Nelken, 2006a). But they can also be complimentary. We could, for example, distinguish among the different tasks of enquiry. If the interpretative approach is an essential step in generating hypotheses and insights, the explanatory approach is the only way we can test their applicability to a wider range of cases. We could also draw on each approach so as to examine variables from more than one point of view. As an explanatory factor, Catholicism in Italy could be treated as an important institution, one that is sometimes united with and sometimes in competition with the political system (as seen, for instance, in its efforts currently to moderate the effort of right-wing governments to criminalise immigrants). But, and at the same time, on an interpretative approach, Catholicism can also be seen as the source of ideals concerning what should be penalised and obligations of tolerance and forgiveness which help shape – or compete with – the ideas developed in the state system.

One author who has recently set out to explain why the criminal justice systems in southern European countries are now sending a disproportionate number of immigrants to prison has demonstrated a statistical correlation between the propensity of immigrants to commit crimes and indicators of the generally poor functioning of local political institutions – as seen in the extent of the black economy and disrespect for law (Solivetti, 2010). But a broader approach to the same issue (apart from bringing in the role of criminal justice institutions themselves) would also seek to grasp the meaning and role of talk about the immigrant crime problem. Thus a book of thoughtful interviews in the Netherlands provide us with a variety of perspectives on why the murders of Pim Fortuyn and Theo van Gogh in the Netherlands had such an impact in such a historically 'tolerant' country and helps us understand why the proportion of immigrants in prison in that country is almost at the level of southern Europe, despite its local institutions being Northern European ones (Baruma, 2006). On the other hand, those interviewed may not be representative, and it can be easy to make too much of them. An interpretative approach should also not distract us from investigating the structural factors linked to problems of integration that can help explain why the number of immigrants in prison is so high in that country.

A related issue that highlights these differences in explanatory approaches is the role of agency as compared to structural constraints in the defining and application of criminal sanctions. At one extreme we have the functionalist approach, which has roots both in social science and comparative law. This treats agency as substantially irrelevant; function does not equal purpose. It invites us to look for the manifest or latent functions of any given element of criminal justice in relation to other elements, to the rest of the legal system, or to the society of which it is part. It explores the way other agencies of social control, from private police to illegal associations such as the *Yakuza* in Japan, serve some of the same functions of the official system (Vagg, 1993), or suggests that the individualising of sentences by judges is *de facto* forestalled by sentencing commissions (Wandall, 2006).

A standard move of comparativists is to ask questions such as what do different jurisdictions use instead of bail to make sure that offenders turn up for trial? Conversely, they may tell us that bail decisions themselves sometimes have other functions. Although judges in 'drug courts' in Ireland cannot bring back cases for review as they do in the USA, they can and do achieve much the same aim through the way they set bail conditions (Nolan, 2009). Even in a regime of obligatory prosecution, decisions or non-decisions on priorities are being made (Nelken and Zanier, 2006). Knowing the answer to such questions is essential if we are to avoid introducing 'reforms' that duplicate or distort already existing local 'best practice' (Feeley, 1983). With some imagination we may also see that what appears at first to be only 'noise', aspects of procedure involving inefficiency and delay, may be playing important functions. (It would be interesting to compare the role of delays in criminal proceedings cases in Italy with those in the USA for death penalty cases).

But functional language, as sociologists have long ago shown, can involve a number of traps. We need, for example, always to ask functional for what, and for whom? The search for 'functional equivalents' has been a matter of fierce controversy in debates over the comparability of continental penal procedures and alleged alternatives to 'plea bargaining' (Langbein and Weinrib, 1978; Volkmann-Schluck, 1981). There is no a priori reason to think that something must be doing a given job – bail or otherwise. Perhaps the news about a given system could be that there is, in fact, no equivalent. It is misleading to assume that modern criminal justice systems all face the same 'problems' even if they deal with them in different ways. 'Problems' – and 'solutions' – are perceived and constructed differently within different cultures. As I wrote soon after moving to Italy:

> Functionalism is a good servant but a poor master. ... Living in another country has given me a jaundiced view of the sort of comparative research which sets out to show that all societies face basically similar problems even if they may solve them in somewhat different ways. What is more striking is the power of culture to produce relatively circular definitions of what is worth fighting for and against and the way institutions and practices express genuinely different histories and distinct priorities. (Nelken, 1992/1996: 356)

I would now add that what culture means can be equally problematic. The strengths and weaknesses of functional explanation can be well illustrated from our running example concerning the rule of obligatory prosecution in Italy. On a functionalist view, it would be assumed that all criminal justice systems of a certain complexity must face similar operational problems of coping with overload and the efficient throughput of cases. Certainly, the Italian criminal justice system faces similar, or even worse, problems of management to those found elsewhere. The criminal law has enormous reach – judges and prosecutors often taking upon themselves the task of 'substituting' for the government where there are insufficient or contradictory signals about how to handle a pressing social problem, for example unaccompanied young immigrants arriving in Italy who are not allowed to work but cannot be expelled.

A function of legally permitted discretionary decision-making is that it makes it easier to manage problems of priorities. We would therefore expect to find that where prosecution discretion is heavily restricted there would be other 'functional equivalents' and we can in fact identify numerous features of the Italian criminal process which do provide the chance to filter out cases or exercise priorities. The threshold decision whether or not there is enough evidence to take a case to trial, or whether instead to opt for what is called *archiviazione*, provided some opportunity for exercise of choice. Another sort of (somewhat random) flexibility is provided by competing and overlapping jurisdictions of types of law and courts and the three stages of trial. The Italian criminal justice system thus has some functional equivalents of discretionary decision-making, though not necessarily where they would be found in other systems. Although little of this would be described in Italy as the exercise of 'discretion', for the sociologist it can be important to discover how flexibility is built into the system and not only how the actors label it.

But we also need to be cautious not to go too far in searching for 'functional equivalents', especially if this is based in the idea that every system is predestined to reach a certain level of efficiency. In Italy even apparently minimal functional operating requirements are not met and it is frequently not easy to determine what is functional and for whom. Many judges and prosecutors believe the courts are underfunded and left dealing with an overload so as to keep them from pursuing politically sensitive matters. The apparently irrational distribution of courts around the country is explained mainly by political pressure not to lose the courthouse as a sign of local prestige. Formalities and complicated division or overlapping of responsibilities help produce enormous delays for which Italy is regularly condemned by the European Court of Human Rights at Strasbourg. The language of functionalism is especially misleading if it suggests that all criminal justice systems operate with a managerial vision of their purposes. This itself varies by culture.

By contrast to most work in the mainstream, interpretative approaches focus more on trying to present a clearer picture of such purposes. They speak of reasons and motives rather than functions and causes and give more importance to agency. They would draw attention to the fact that politicians, in the UK, such as Margaret Thatcher and Tony Blair, had characteristic ways of approaching the issue of crime, and that Douglas Hurd, the mandarin Tory minister (the Home Secretary), who was responsible for criminal justice matters in the 1990s, relied heavily on policy advice from his senior civil servants, whereas Michael Howard, a later successor, took a more populist approach, insisting on the basis of his own reading of the evidence – that 'prison works'. In Italy, many 'reforms' of criminal procedure were directly connected to Berlusconi's attempt to extricate himself from pending court proceedings.

Other individuals can also make a difference (think of Darrel Vandeveld, the catholic prosecutor who resigned rather than continue to be involved as military prosecutor in the trials in Guantanamo). But agency is not just a matter of named individuals. In Italy, the organised left-leaning group of judges *Magistratura Democratica* sees itself as playing a vital role in defending what it calls *jurisdizione* from political threats. Reductions in prison rates in other countries have been attributed to decisions of bureaucratic elites, as in post-Second World War Finland (Van Hofer, 2003; Lappi-Seppala, 2007). Vice versa, the growth in incarceration rates in other countries is attributed to the 'fall of the Platonic guardians' (Loader, 2006), such as the reduced reliance by ministers in England and Wales on senior civil servants in the Home Office (Ministry of Justice), even if this has also been seen as greater democratic responsiveness (Ryan, 2003).

For many of those who use interpretative approaches, it is only by finding out what criminal justice actors and others actually think they are doing that we can make sense of it. As West puts it, 'to understand scandal cross-culturally we need some way of exploring people's belief about it' (West, 2009: 4). But interpretative approaches do not have to limit themselves to this. Jim Whitman, for example, in his interesting study of relative leniency in punishment in Continental Europe describes the 'structures of feeling' that derive from egalitarian and inegalitarian social orders (Whitman, 2003). At the same time, however, he rejects explanations offered by some of his interviewees who attributed leniency in Europe to the experience of having been German prisoners of war or in concentration camps.

On culture and concepts

An obvious route to making sense of differences in criminal justice practices would seem to lie in the idea of culture, seen as a historically shaped sets of habits, understandings, values and priorities that shape or exemplify what societies choose to sanction and how they do so (e.g. Karstedt, 2008). Thus the textbooks tell us that the fact that in Japan prosecutors dismiss many cases is affirmation of their Japanese 'norm of avoidance'

of formal judicial processes (Dammer, Fairchild and Albanese, 2005: 157). As often, however, culture is contrasted with instrumentality. Some writers conclude that on the continent judicial supervision is only 'a myth', or claim that terms such as 'zero tolerance' have 'only' symbolic importance. A more culturalist perspective would stress that there are few things more important than myths and symbols as a way of creating identity, expressing commitment and serving as regulatory ideals.

'Legal culture' (Friedman, 1975), a term that focuses on legal aspects of culture, may be of particular relevance for the study of comparative criminal justice. I have elsewhere redefined this term for comparative purposes as

> one way of describing relatively stable patterns of legally-oriented social behaviour and attitudes. The identifying elements of legal culture range from facts about institutions such as the number and role of lawyers, or the ways judges are appointed and controlled, to various forms of behaviour, such as litigation or prison rates, and, at the other extreme, more nebulous aspects of ideas, values, aspirations and mentalities. Like culture itself, legal culture is about who we are, not just what we do. (Nelken, 2004a: 1)

Using this idea could help us decide what sense to give to the idea of criminal justice as a set of supposedly interconnected legal decisions. Cross-culturally, 'criminal justice' may not always be the term used to get at this, but in most systems the various actors involved are likely to claim that there ought to be some overall coherence to these decisions. What is certain is that, wherever one looks, decisions at one point have implications for others (with consequences that are sometimes unintended). Abolish capital punishment and the use of prison is likely to go up, reduce police discretion and more falls to the prosecution. The various features of criminal justice in Italy that we have been discussing also interact. For example, the way prosecutors implement the rule of obligatory prosecution can lead to counter-intuitive outcomes in practice. The length of time before a case becomes time-bound (i.e. prescribed) is statutorily related to the gravity of offence – the more serious the offence, the more time is available. Under orders (from either or both the head of the office and the ministry) not to allow cases to become time-bound, prosecutors therefore often feel the need to focus their effort on *less* serious cases with impending prescription dates, rather than more serious cases which have longer times still to run (Nelken and Zanier, 2006). When prosecutors increase their speed of throughput a new bottleneck appears at the stage of court hearings (Sarzotti, 2008).

A useful distinction made by Friedman is that between 'internal legal culture', the ideas and practices of those working for or within the legal system, and 'external legal culture', the opinions, actions and pressures brought to bear on law by those outside it. This could be helpful in exploring differences in the involvement of lay people in the system of criminal justice, or the significance attached to surveys of public attitudes to sentencing and of the fear of crime. The respect in which internal legal culture is open to external legal culture is a key aspect of criminal justice. If we want to understand why practices such as victim–offender mediation have had less fortune in some countries in Continental Europe than in Anglo-American type jurisdictions, we have to take into account, *inter alia*, the way the European 'state' project limits the kind of role individual victims are expected to play in the criminal process (Crawford, 2000a). In Japan, whose borrowing of the continental model reinforced its top-down approach, internal legal culture has been, until recently, relatively immune to public opinion. According to David Johnson: the lack of external pressures clearly privileges 'internal legal culture', the ideas, values, expectations and attitudes that prosecutors have about criminal law, behaviour and justice. But the ideas mobilised by prosecutors – and others in the legal system – also relate to wider aspects of Japanese culture. Johnson attributes particular significance to the Japanese belief that human nature is perfectible, in contrast to the Christian doctrine of original sin (Johnson, 2000).

But terms like 'culture' and 'legal culture' are highly controversial (Nelken, 2006d, 2007b). It is often objected that explaining behaviour by reference to culture tends to assume that it is determining, bounded and unchanging. As compared to seeing it as the 'cause' of certain behaviours, it is usually better to see culture as a matter of struggle and disagreement. The purported uniformity, coherence or stability of given national cultures will often be no more than a rhetorical claim projected by outside observers, or manipulated by elements within the culture concerned. Much that goes under the name of culture is no more – but also no less – than 'imagined communities' or 'invented traditions' (but again these may of course be real in their effects). It is essential to avoid reifying national stereotypes. Think, for example, of the transformations in elite attitudes towards 'law and order' from Weimar to Hitlerian Germany. Because of their all-embracing referents, cultural explanations run a serious risk of tautology.

Should we define culture as 'attitudes, beliefs and values' and see practices as what result from these? This works better when explaining a single system as opposed to comparing systems. How should we demarcate legal culture from what else is going on? How, if at all, can we draw a line between legal culture and 'institutions' (Brants and Field, 2000) or 'structures' (Nelken, 2006a). The pioneering work of David Downes on Dutch tolerance shows us that as social structure (the system of political coordination known as 'pillarism') changed, so did cultural attitudes to inclusion (Downes, 1988, 2010; Downes and Van Swaaningen, 2007). On the other hand, culture can also explain the lack of change. There are ironic continuities in the way attempts to purify the state of communism in Poland (in the name of religious and patriotic values) relied on patterns of prosecution which were very similar to those used under communism (Polak and Nelken, 2010).

Not surprisingly, reference to culture tends to reproduce the division between explanation and interpretation we have been discussing so far (and different social science disciplines, such as political science and anthropology, also tend to treat it in correspondingly different ways). We can use culture to explain differences (Hofstede, 1980) or we can seek to explain culture itself. Treated as an explanatory variable, culture may be relevant in some cases more than others. As Johnson writes:

In one sense everything is culture, but with respect to capital punishment that approach may not shed much insight on some questions we consider important, such as: why China is the world's execution leader, or why 'other Chinas' such as Hong Kong and Taiwan have such different death penalty policies compared to the PRC, or why North and South Korea have such wildly different death penalty policies, or why Hong Kong evidenced no backlash against the stoppage of executions or the abolition of capital punishment, or why Singapore went through a huge execution surge and then a 90% drop in the course of only 15 years, etc. (Johnson, email to me, 21/2/2009)

The interpretative approach, by contrast, treats culture less as a variable than as part of a flow of meaning, 'the enormous interplay of interpretations in and about a culture' (Friedman, 1994: 73) to which social actors, including scholars, also contribute. On this perspective, cultural sensibilities, a result of historical contingencies and collective experiences and memories, support (or can be made to support) some action strategies and delegitimate others. Christopher Birkbeck has pointed to fundamental differences between the meaning of prisons in North and South America, making reference, *inter alia*, to contrasts in the idea of prison as a warehouse and in the concept of 'doing time' (Birkbeck and Pérez-Santiago, 2006; Birkbeck, forthcoming). More generally, scholars explore the different meanings of the 'Rule of law', the '*Rechtsstaat*', and the '*Stato di diritto*', relate Italian '*garantismo*' to English 'due process', or 'law and order' to the German '*innere sicherheit*', or probe the meaning of '*lokale justiz*' as contrasted to 'community crime control' (Zedner, 1995).

Even the local idiom may be complex. Edwards and Hughes note that 'crime', 'harm', 'safety' and 'security' might be used interchangeably in English-language policy and academic discourse, but they often 'signify competing political constructs of what constitutes order' (Edwards and Hughes, 2005: 346). In Italy, until very recently, the expression adopted both in newspapers and academic discussions to describe conventional crimes, including even burglary, rape and robbery, was the term '*microcriminality*'. This was contrasted with corruption, terrorism and organised crime, which threatened the state itself – these were the implicit but never so denominated macro-crimes. Largely as a result of becoming a country of immigration, there is now less tolerance of micro-crime and the term increasingly being substituted is the Italian equivalent of 'street crime' or 'diffuse crime'. Likewise, the past shadows the present. In Italy, in the spring of 2009, as part of a new law on security, there was much discussion of what role could be found for local-level citizens patrols acting in concert with the municipal police. The junior political ally in Berlusconi's coalition, the Northern Leagues, was pressing for them to be introduced in the areas under their control. They were happy for them to be called '*le ronde*' despite the term's fascist connotations. But Berlusconi himself expressed a wish that a different name could be found to describe the same thing, and proposed 'associations'.

The interaction between relatively standardised and more local terms can be a valuable area of research. For example, in comparing Italy and the UK, the concept of trust – 'whom do you trust, when do you trust, how do you trust, how much do you trust' – can frame a series of issues about variation in matters relevant to criminal justice without using terms from given domestic systems. It could help explain and measure a range of differences. For example, why it tends to be easier to get a job in the UK and the USA, but also easier to lose one as compared to Continental Europe, or the ease of collaboration between official agencies as compared to the crime world itself. But at the same time such an approach needs to be accompanied by an exploration of the local meanings of the word *fiducia* (trust), as seen, for example, in Italian proverbs about the risks of trusting (Nelken, 1994b).

On the other hand, terms with wider currency can be emptied of or changed in their meaning in local contexts. Take the requirement of the 'independence' of judges from political control. In the early post-2000 period, the so-called 'law and justice' governing party in Poland, despite its name, was seen as representing a threat to the autonomy of legal institutions. In recent interviews concerning the autonomy of prosecutors in Poland in dealing with corruption, we were informed in the course of our research that the local quip was that 'prosecutors' independence means that nothing depends on the prosecutor' (Polak and Nelken, 2010). Terms can also live on, zombie-like, when taken out of their usual context, or perhaps given new life, as when the idea of prison as a place for re-socialisation is endorsed by transnational bodies even though abandoned by some of the national prison administrations they are monitoring.

Whether terms have cross-national applicability has both intellectual and political implications. In his efforts to build global legal theory with concepts that can have purchase transnationally, William Twining contrasts the terms used in the fight against corruption with those used to criticise and raise the standards of prison conditions worldwide. Whereas definitions of corruption have only imperfect cross-cultural applicability, there has been more success in finding a common language for talking about prisoners' rights (Twining, 2005). One reason for this, he suggests, could be that the modern prison, as an institution, diffused out from a common origin in the USA. While we can agree in principle that some concepts may, as Twining says, 'travel well' as compared to others, any given example of this can be controversial. In fact, Transparency International seems to be quite successful in imposing some sort of common definition of corruption, while, conversely, Birkbeck claims that prison has quite a different meaning in North and South America (Birkbeck, forthcoming; Nelken, forthcoming b). Even concepts that have no readily obvious local meaning can somehow get domesticated, as when the sentencing reform based on the idea of 'three strikes and you are out' is proposed in places that don't play much baseball! (Jones and Newburn, 2008).

Wider and more local terms are thus not insulated from each other, and scholars are among those who play a major and consequential role in bringing about their mutual interaction. The influential criminological notion of 'moral panic' (Cohen, 1972), used to describe alleged repressive over-reaction to deviant behaviour, has by now spread across Europe and been applied in literature describing increasing concerns about street crime in Scandinavia, Spain, Italy, Greece and Japan. The local Italian term *'allarme sociale'* may be subtly different, conjuring up as it does less a disproportionate reaction to a threat than the need felt by professionals in the legal system to keep distance from emotional over-reactions. But increasingly the two terms are merging. The Japanese have two words for scandal: *shuba*, meaning disgusting news, and *sukyandaru*, essentially an imported word designed to capture Western meanings (West, 2009: 7). If people in Russia learn to think of the policing they experience as 'predatory policing', their attitude to the police is likely to change (Gerber and Mendelson, 2008).

The Italian examples that I have been using in this book also illustrate the need for interpretation, as well as the challenges of invoking culture (and legal culture) in understanding systems of criminal justice. Take the measure which means that young people (in a sense) 'get away with murder'. The ministerial website proudly speaks of near 80 per cent success of the *messa alla prova* pre-trial probation disposal used for these and other crimes, and urges all juvenile courts to make more use of it. But it is not referring to the internationally standardised criterion of a two-year period of non-offending following a disposal, but only to the number of cases that are held to have been a success by the judges at the end of the measure itself. In practice it is only in the most serious cases of non-compliance with this measure that a judge will decide on holding a trial, the outcome of which could only be, if conviction follows, prison or, more likely, suspended prison. Whatever positive good the juvenile justice system has to provide is only on offer in pre-trial probation. So judges are reluctant to find that youngsters have failed. By contrast, the only published attempt in Italy to measure young offender's recidivism after this disposal, albeit only in one court district in northern Italy, came up with a rate of over 40 per cent. Perhaps still acceptable, but a somewhat different outcome.

Culture is relevant to all three of the running examples I have been discussing. The principles adopted in the Italian juvenile justice system have to do with the wider culture of the late 1980s, but they also reflect more basic features of social structure that help explain why political pressure for change has not been able to overcome the resistance of those in favour of the current system. The attachment to obligatory prosecution, apart from being enshrined in the constitution, also reflects a cultural preoccupation, this time with the risks of personal or politicised decision-making. But its survival is now in doubt as recent Italian governments of the centre-right try to change the status of prosecutors by distinguishing them more sharply from judges and, more subtly, by detaching the loyalties of the police that prosecutors need to use in their tasks. Court delays, finally, parallel other cultural patterns which privilege procedure over substance. But they also ensure that – at least in the short and medium term – it is usually more rational for an individual to rely on existing forms of clientalist dependence rather than turn to legal remedies.

FOUR

explaining too much?

The major current debate in comparative criminal justice has to do with how best to explain the current growth in so-called 'punitiveness' – or willingness to punish – as evidenced especially in the rise in imprisonment rates. It has generated a considerable literature, to which I shall only be able to make limited reference here. But this chapter is in any case intended less to contribute to this debate than to comment on it. I seek to throw further light on some of the central questions in comparative criminal justice that I have been discussing so far – the differences between the tasks of description, explanation and interpretation, the part played by criminal procedure in explaining penal outcomes, the problems of comparing like with like and, not least, the dangers of ethnocentrism.

The debate over punitiveness

The puzzle at the heart of this chapter is well captured by leading penologist Michael Tonry when he writes that: 'punishment and crime have little to do with each other. That observation is a commonplace for most European criminologists, some North American criminologists, and very few politicians' (Tonry, 2005). In their search for comparable data, scholars of comparative criminal justice have been among the pioneers of those seeking to obtain a more faithful picture about crime levels through asking samples of potential victims in different countries to report their experiences, rather than relying on the cases that happen to get recorded in official statistics (Van Dijk et al., 2007). Their findings show that punishment has continued to rise even when crime levels are decreasing and that, cross-nationally, the levels of crime and punishment do not correlate well.

Apart from victim surveys, other methods also show that, recently, punishment has been rising while crime has remained stable. For example, Felipe Estrada ingeniously demonstrated that the nature of injuries in crime incidents reported in hospital casualty rooms in Stockholm stayed the same even as police definition of such injuries became more serious, hence leading to greater punishment (Estrada, 2006). Though less stressed at the present time, the opposite is also true. Punishment levels do not always follow rising crime. As late as 1990, scholars of comparative criminal justice described the dominant trend as one towards more lenient punishment and the 'defining-down' of deviance (Haferkampf and Ellis, 1992). Before taking Tonry's words literally (or out of context), however, more would need to be said about the opposite question of possible effects of changes in punishment on crime levels. Few criminologists would deny that there is some relationship, even if it is far from linear. Nonetheless, almost all criminologists agree that – even in the USA – only a small part of the recent reduction in crime can be attributed to the increasing use of prison.

Comparison of the willingness to punish between states within the USA, as well as between nation-states, has a long pedigree. Paradoxically, however, the recent stimulus to comparative work came about in large part because of the influential analysis offered by David Garland of the connections between the rise of punishment and widespread late-modern changes in social and economic conditions, including exposure of the middle classes to 'high crime' rates (Garland, 2001). Garland offered a rich, but pessimistic, account of the way 'penal welfarism' had been displaced by the politicisation of crime and the growth of popular punitiveness. He noted, for example, the privileging of public protection and the claim that 'prison works', and described the changes in the emotional tone of crime policy from decency and humanity to insecurity, anger and resentment. But he gave little attention to differences between countries. Thus the question arose: did his analysis hold generally? There is some evidence that the thesis is widely applicable, or at least (what is not exactly the same thing) that 'the culture of control' is spreading like a firestorm (Waquant, 2009a). For example, the Netherlands, once a 'beacon of tolerance', is seen as going in this direction (Downes and Van Swaaningen, 2007; Downes, 2010). And even Japan is now changing its criminal justice system to respond to political and popular calls for more severity (Fenwick, 2005; Miyazawa, 2008).

But others deny that there has been any such general turn to punitiveness and argue that we can and must avoid assuming that Europe is also bound to end up with something like the American dystopia, with its bloated penal system that now embraces more than two million prisoners (Zedner, 2002). In Ireland, to take only one example, the use of prison was eight times higher in the 1950s than fifty years later (O'Sullivan and O'Donnell, 2007). Nor is there any earlier golden age to set against the present once we take into account that 'welfare' in the context of criminal justice is also a form of social control (Mathews, 2005) and that it still forms a central part of current 'volatile and contradictory' practices (O'Malley, 1999). Tonry himself insists that '(m)any of the generalizations bandied about in discussions of penal policy in Western countries are not true'. Populism or populist punitiveness, if it exists at all, he says, 'is mostly as reifications in academics' minds of other academics' ideas'. Imprisonment rates have not risen substantially everywhere in the last fifteen years. Some penal policies in some places have become harsher, but in most places this is offset by changes in practice that moderate and sometimes nullify the policy changes, and by other policy changes that move in the opposite direction (Tonry, 2007a: 1).

From this perspective, what Garland and others are describing is something principally tied to the political and legal culture of the USA. What we need to explore are the differences between the USA and Europe, and even within Europe, differences that suggest that there are multiple *cultures of control* rather than just one 'culture of control' (Pratt et al., 2005). Certainly the numbers in prison in the US are out of all proportion to other Western countries, even if the rise of the prison archipelago is fundamentally a phenomenon of the last thirty years and there are enormous differences even now between some of its constituent states and others (Hinds, 2005; Newburn, 2006). Explanatory factors that are particularly relevant to the USA range from the importance of racial divisions, the history of the frontier, attitudes to gun owner- ship, the role of elected judges and prosecutors, the need for politicians such as state governors to take a hard line against crime so as to have a chance of getting into power, and the influence of single-issue pressure groups at the federal level. The absence of such factors helps explain why other places have less people in prison. In addition, in explaining why other countries have lower prison rates, we must consider their 'shields' against punitiveness. There seems to be a strong link between the level of social inequality and (other) negative social consequences (Wilkinson, 1996). Savelsberg offers a triangular comparison of the USA, West Germany and Poland that highlights the role of strong state bureaucracies, centralised and decentralised administration of justice, and institutions of knowledge production and diffusion (Savelsberg, 1994, 1999).

The political economy of punitiveness

But the debate on which factors are the key to explaining punitiveness is far from settled. In the rest of this chapter I offer a critical discussion of just one recent contribution to this debate. In their innovative work, Cavadino and Dignan try to straddle generalising and particularising approaches so as to explain both why punitiveness has been growing and why it is by no means a uniform development (Cavadino and Dignan, 2006a, 2006b). Their argument has been much praised by other lead- ing writers in Great Britain, who, like them, are also concerned to stop the dangerous slide in England and Wales towards an ever-expanding prison system. In the rest of this chapter I first summarise their claims, then consider what their comparison holds 'constant', and the plau- sibility of the independent and dependent variables that make up the structure of their explanation. I then go on to argue for the need for a more interpretative approach to notions such as punitiveness and tolerance.

Cavadino and Dignan reject common-sense explanations such as differences in crime levels or in public attitudes towards sentences as the reason for variations in prison rates. Instead, they build on prior neo-Marxist analyses of the role of the prison in relation to the labour force (for a recent example, see De Georgi, 2007), as well as classifications of welfare typologies in the social policy literature, claiming that political economy, and in particular the influence of neo-liberalism, offers the key to differences in punitiveness as measured by the numbers of people in prison. I have reproduced in Table 4.1 the data that they see as supporting their thesis. This shows us that the rates in twelve modern industrial societies vary considerably and consistently between what they call neo-liberal, conservative-corporatist, social-democratic and oriental-corporatist types of political economy. The updating of their figures (the numbers in brackets) also indicates that these striking differences have remained pretty stable over the past few years.

Table 4.1　Imprisonment rates per 100,000 in 12 countries (2002/03[1] and 2008[2])

Neo-liberal countries	
USA	701 (756)
South Africa	402 (334)
New Zealand	155 (185)
England and Wales	141 (152)
Australia	115 (129)
Conservative-corporatist countries	
Italy	100 (92)
Germany	98 (89)
The Netherlands	100 (100)
France	93 (96)
Social-democratic countries	
Sweden	73 (74)
Finland	70 (64)
Oriental-corporatist countries	
Japan	53 (63)

[1] Source: Cavadino and Dignan, 2006a: 22.
[2] The figures in brackets are updated from those in their book.
Source: www.kcl.ac.UK/depsta/law/research/icps/worldbrief/
wpb_stats.php (accessed 12/01/2010). See the latest figures at the
site of the International Centre for Prison Studies.

At the risk of over-simplification, their claim can be summarised as follows. Neo-liberal societies have the highest prison rates because they follow social and economic policies that lead to what they describe as '*exclusionary* cultural attitudes towards our deviant and marginalised fellow citizens' (Cavadino and Dignan, 2006a: 23. Emphasis added). On the other hand, Continental European corporatist societies and, even more, Scandinavia social-democratic societies, 'pursue more *inclusive* economic and social policies that give citizens more protection from unfettered market forces'. These societies 'see offenders as needing resocialisation which is the responsibility of the community as a whole' (Cavadino and Dignan, 2006a: 24 Emphasis added) Stated like this, Cavadino and Dignan's thesis fits well into the mainstream style of explanatory work in comparative criminal justice that tries to tie together explanatory variables and punishment outcomes. Their book, however, also draws on the views of selected locally-based experts so as fill in what they call missing 'idiosyncratic' detail. But they conclude that this does not require them to modify their overall thesis.

Cavadino and Dignan, like most of those comparing a large range of incarceration rates, spend little time on persuading us that crime rates are really the same in all the countries they are comparing. But it is this, the assumption that crime levels are 'constant' in the places being compared, that sets the puzzle they are trying to solve. How can some societies live with high crime rates without concomitant expansion of the prison realm? If countries with higher prison rates were actually dealing with higher threats from crime, this would not be news, and we could hardly say that we were fairly comparing levels of *punitiveness*. (Rather, we would be showing how neo-liberalism increases both crime and punishment.) On the other hand, it is strange that the good things about more inclusive welfare-oriented or egalitarian social-democratic societies do not also reduce the level, or severity, of crimes being committed, rather than only shaping the response to them. And since our ideal is presumably to live in places that have both low levels of punishment and low crime it is a pity that this inconvenient point is passed over so quickly.

In fact, there are reasons to think that some of the places in their table with higher prison rates do have higher levels of crime. The USA certainly has more lethal violence than any of the other countries in their list and South Africa too suffers exceptional levels of homicide, violence and rape. Victim surveys show that England and Wales has higher rates of burglary. One comparison of overall victimisation rates for ten crimes places England and Wales top, with the Scandinavian countries and Japan the lowest (Van Dijk, 2007: 158). As with all official statistics, what lies behind and produces overall prison rates needs to be studied empirically and carefully disentangled. It is important to see who is in prison, for what crimes, and how they arrived there. Many of the countries that have lower rates, Sweden for example, or Switzerland, or the Netherlands in its glorious period, use shorter prison terms but actually send relatively *more* people to prison than those with higher overall rates. Does this show less punitiveness than sending fewer people for longer periods? It certainly complicates any argument we may want to make about punitiveness and inclusiveness.

According to the 2006 figures, Italy had the lowest prison population among the larger European countries. But the explanation for this does not lie with the generosity of its welfare or work training systems (welfare payments mainly go to pay pensions). It owed everything to an *indulto* or collective pardon, which freed over a third of its prison inmates just before the Council of Europe collected its data. Its prison population is now again rising and is predicted to reach pre-*indulto* levels shortly. This may be a particularly striking example, but it can be difficult, perhaps even fruitless, to try to purify comparative figures of such external interventions. Finland which, post-Second World War, had one of the highest prison rates, deliberately brought its figures down so as to be more in line with its Scandinavian neighbours (Von Hofer, 2003). Such volatility is not easy to reconcile with claims about the dependence of prison rates on underlying basic differences in political economy.

Cavadino and Dignan's thesis about neo-liberalism is certainly a plausible candidate to be part of the explanation for the recent increase in prison rates, as well as a factor in explaining differences between places. But their argument may not apply so well outside the range of countries they compare. There are countries (such as China) which make a high use of prison without being neo-liberal, and others, such as Russia or South Africa, where moves towards neo-liberalism have actually gone together with some reduction in the use of prison. This suggests that a wider variety of variables than those connected to political economy may also lead to high or lower punitiveness. More interesting, perhaps, in relation to the countries they selected, it could also be argued that their explanation risks being tautological, showing that it may not always be easy to draw a line between classification, description and the allegedly more powerful strategy of explanation. It is hardly surprising to find that neo-liberalism in the USA and Europe correlates with exclusionary attitudes towards offenders, given that Cavadino and Dignan themselves *actually define neo-liberalism as including such attitudes*, as well as justifying the diversion of spending from welfare to the criminal justice system (Cavadino and Dignan, 2006b: 15, Table 1). They explain that there are differences between the countries they compare in terms of two other dependent variables: the degree to which they have private prisons and the age of onset of criminal responsibility. But again, it could be objected that the former factor is just another expression of neo-liberalism and even the latter has to do with the individualism that is an ingredient of all forms of liberalism.

For some commentators, other independent variables need to be added to those identified by Cavadino and Dignan. Lacey (2008), for example, fully accepts that what she calls 'societies with coordinated market economies' are indeed less punitive. But she argues that we should also consider the way multi-party political systems with proportional voting see less resort to populist politics than two-party systems, and rightly recommends that we take into account the influence of the long-established constitutional and legal frameworks in which criminal justice systems are embedded. Lacey admits, however, that the specificities of different societies can cause problems for her thesis. New Zealand has one of the harshest penal dispensations despite its multi-party system. And once we recognise that different variables may be relevant in different societies, a table comparing prison rates can easily obscure as much as it reveals. Some of the Scandinavian countries with low prison rates have experienced little immigration; others even have long-standing blocks on economic migration. Can this be ignored?

Are the Netherlands and Italy really similarly punitive – and for similar reasons of political economy? What of social control outside criminal justice? Not for nothing, Cavadino and Dignan entitle their chapter on Japan 'Iron fist in a velvet glove'. As far as the Italian case is concerned,

Cavadino and Dignan are right to stress the importance of corporatist rather than market structures. But it could be just as important to think about religion. Likewise there is the continuing centrality in Italy not only of the family and extended family, especially important with respect to the handling of juvenile delinquency, but also of family-like groups in maintaining social order in many sectors of public and private life. Some of those helping to maintain 'order' in the southern regions (and hence keeping prison rates low) are actually criminal groups.

For Tonry himself, it is politics with all its contradictions, rather than political economy, that is the master variable, both for explaining America's exceptional prison rates and differences within Europe (Tonry, 2001, 2007a). Certainly, if we again consider the Italian case, politics seems a very significant variable. Few national politicians (other than those on the far right) sought in the past to exploit populist fear about crime for electoral advantage in the face of their own vulnerability to prosecution, the widespread popular distrust of the state, and reluctance to see it as too powerful. There is also, not least, the somewhat different status of victims in a Catholic country where they are expected to forgive more than to authorise revenge. But the independent variable that most directly explains Cavadino and Dignan's findings, in Italy and elsewhere, is to be found not at the level of the wider society and its politics but in the quotidian practices shaped by criminal procedure. All systems of criminal justice are to some degree intended to be selective in the cases that are taken on to trial and penalty, but they differ among themselves (and over time) in the way they construct and operate such selectivity. In Italy, for example, it is the attrition rate of cases as they go through the long and complex requirements of criminal procedure that is particularly striking.

As the three aspects of Italian penal procedure that I have been using as running examples well illustrate, many cases start out but few arrive at a conclusion. The 1989 innovations in juvenile justice procedure were brought in as a way of holding up trial. Obligatory prosecution too can end up contributing to court delays and cases becoming 'prescribed' and thus time-bound. And court delay speaks for itself. The typical procedural guarantees of the adversarial system (centring on the forensic contest of the trial) that were introduced in the principal 1989 reform of criminal procedure, were simply added to the ones that belong to the inquisitorial tradition. Even quite minor cases go through a series of procedural hoops and are reviewed by a large number of judges, and there are two stages of appeal (the first stage being a retrial on the facts). There are complex rules about informing the accused and his lawyers of trial hearings at each stage of the proceedings and extensive periods are allowed for them to prepare their defence each time. It is not infrequent for such notifications to go astray, especially where there is more than one accused and lawyer involved. Uniquely, the so-called 'prescription', statute of limitations period, after which criminal proceedings become null and void, continues to run until the Cassation court has given its final verdict. On the other hand, illegal immigrants, especially those 'caught in the act' of committing crimes, are unable to take advantage of many of the routine procedural benefits of the system, and it is these, mainly property offenders, who, together with low-level drug dealers, now tend to fill the prisons.

But is Italy just a special case? (As Mrs Thatcher liked to say, when characterising various countries in the European Union, 'and then there's Italy'). Its politics may be somewhat unusual, but criminal procedure and case attrition is also a large part of the explanation of how other countries with low prison rates kept them low in the past, or still do so. Germany, for example, diverts around half of its prosecutions, and France in the 1980s and 1990s repeatedly resorted to amnesties as a response to prison overcrowding (Lévy, 2007; Roche, 2007). The Netherlands and Switzerland used to send offenders home to wait until places were ready for them in prison. Yet the more we emphasise the role of criminal procedure as an explanation in its own right, the more it becomes difficult to draw a line between independent variables and the dependent variable – prison rates – that independent variables are intended to explain. In fact, it has been argued that the whole basis of relying on incarceration rates as measures of punitiveness is simply mistaken and it only makes sense to compare prison rates per number of people actually prosecuted (Pease, 1994).

On the other hand, the importance of socio-political variables could be reaffirmed by arguing that criminal procedure merely represents the *means* used to express underlying leniency (and similar issues of 'why' versus 'how' could of course also be raised regarding other variables, for example the role of the media.) What happens within the criminal justice system is certainly often linked to other aspects of political and social structure, even if this may not be easy to grasp without some inside knowledge. Lacey, for example, suggests that in Europe it is collaboration between politicians, policy-makers and courts that keeps prison rates down (Lacey, 2008). But Italian experience suggests that it can be refusal of such collaboration that leads to the same result, as many judges and prosecutors seek to resist efforts by politicians to encourage the mass criminalisation of illegal immigrants (Montana and Nelken, forthcoming). As this suggests, it is best to see criminal procedure as a semi-autonomous variable in its own right, constraining as well as being shaped by larger factors. There are crucial differences between common law and continental countries with regard to how far *it is thought right* for criminal justice to be insulated or responsive to political direction or to social expectations. And it is the breaking down of such ideas about autonomy that is bringing about change in Europe and Japan.

The meanings of tolerance

Whatever difficulties there may be in correctly identifying the relevant *independent* variables that can explain variations in punitiveness and tolerance, it can be even more important to think about the cross-national meaning of *dependent* variables such as punitiveness, leniency and tolerance. What turns punishment into punitiveness? Are we talking of neutral 'facts' or of value judgements, and whose judgements count or should count? Can there be too little punishment? Is tolerance always good? To what sort of behaviour are these terms being applied? It has been argued that, in late modernity, tolerance for some kinds of deviance (for example, sexual deviance) may have increased, but that there is now less willingness to reform and reintegrate those who engage in offending (Young, 1999). In the Netherlands the differences between the two kinds of tolerance and the way they have evolved recently is well evidenced by the late Pim Fortuyn's flamboyant display of an alternative sexual lifestyle combined with his insistence on the threat represented by Muslim immigration.

But there are important variations in this process from place to place, with Scandinavian countries currently tending to integrate offenders but moralise about deviance, and disapproval of offending may often be a covert way of refusing difference.

Are punishment and tolerance on the same or on different continua? Is tolerance the name we give to the outcome of intentional choices, for example the willingness to organise welfare interventions? Or is it an alternative to such interventions – just the name we give to deliberate or even negligent non-enforcement of available sanctions? If punitiveness and tolerance are deliberate strategies, who is it that is pursuing them – politicians, legal professionals, the public – or all of these? How do they influence each other? Can we speak sensibly about punitiveness and tolerance in different cultures without specifying what the actors in each of the societies concerned mean by these terms? Admittedly, this is not the only approach we can take. If we are imposing judgements from the outside, it could be acceptable to describe behaviour as more or less punitive – just as we can say behaviour is more or less racist – even if the actors would not necessarily recognise such a description of their behaviour. But Cavadino and Dignan offer their analysis as an attempt to grasp what those involved think they are trying to achieve. Can it be irrelevant that what I call tolerance you call permissiveness, indulgence, favouritism, neglect, indifference, impunity, denial or collusion (Nelken, 2006a, 2006b)? What if tolerance of others committing crime is a result of a lack of civicness and minding one's own business?

There is a very large literature on public attitudes to crime (see e.g. Beckett, 1997; Roberts and Hough, 2005). Cavadino and Dignan, however, rule out the obvious short-cut of arguing that it is simply differences in public attitudes to criminals that provides the explanation of differences in incarceration rates. They provide a table that relates the punitiveness scores of the general public (measured by whether the sentence they consider the appropriate punishment for a crime coincides with that typically imposed by the courts) to the position of the country concerned in the rank order of those sending offenders to prison (Cavadino and Dignan, 2006b: 30, Table 1.3). This throws up some problem cases. The public in Japan is more punitive than the typical sentences handed down, whereas people in New Zealand or France are less so. But even if the correlation between public attitudes and the incarceration rate is not perfect, in most of the countries in their list public expectations and court sentences are in fact roughly in line with each other. Van Dijk, too, argues 'in the western world, the countries where the public clearly favours imprisonment, such as the USA and the UK, tend to have comparatively higher prisoners rates' (Van Dijk, 2007: 150–1; see also Solivetti, 2010).

The question remains where these attitudes come from. Do they produce harshness or result from it? At the level of elites there is some evidence that the creation of punitive outcomes can be more or less intentional. From their public pronouncements it would seem that many leaders in the USA are against 'forgiveness' and politicians there and in the UK are less concerned with keeping prison rates down than with finding ways of reducing crime and problematic behaviour. Italians, on the other hand, were leaders in the international decarceration movement (which aimed to have mental patients and others treated in the community rather than in total institutions). In general political discussions, Italian commentators do speak a great deal about 'solidarity' as a way of referring to inclusion. But, in the context of criminal justice, they tend to speak less about being 'tolerant' than of the need to subject the criminal process to strict procedural requirements or *garanzie*.

As elsewhere, however, there is now rising criticism (mobilised both by some politicians and parts of the media) of the 'tolerance' of everyday crime that is consequent on attrition in the penal process. Notice is drawn to the 'inexplicable' way in which even alleged serious criminals can find themselves still at large while awaiting trial, or benefit in other ways from what seem like excessive procedural formalities. Such rethinking is seen in the increasing currency of terms like *buonismo* (pretentious generosity at others' expense), *perdonismo* (being too ready to forgive everything), or *garanzie pelose* (so-called 'hairy' procedural guarantees that are seen as measures pretending to protect the rights of the accused, but really aiming to create a system whereby it will be possible, if needed, to get certain accused people off the hook at all costs).

As this reminds us, an investigation of local concepts can provide clues to differences in approaches to punitiveness. What the Dutch call *gedogen*, or guided tolerance, does not correspond to the English term 'tolerance' because that can also be passive whereas the Dutch concept refers to an open-eyed tolerance – a matter of government policy. In Italy, on the other hand, the state could never explicitly approve such accommodation because of the fear that the law will then be bent to the interests of those who wish to achieve immunity for their own misdeeds while targeting their opponents. Italy's inclusiveness thus has less to do with the guiding role of the regulatory state than it does with attitudes of low respect for the legality mandated by the national state, combined with a cultural emphasis on forgiveness, solidarity and fraternalism deriving from current local interpretations of a strong Catholic heritage and left-wing ideologies. 'Tolerance' as non-enforcement comes about *de facto* because the legislative body tends to multiply offences at the same time as doing nothing about the considerable difficulties that exist when it comes to enforcing them. Sometimes government impotence may also merge into collusion with elite crime – what has been described as 'ruling through leniency' (Melossi, 1994). Sometimes, laxity in enforcing rules and readiness to accept amends after the event is used as a way of currying popular support.

Could such differences sustain the claims of cultural relativism? We are told, for example, that the term *gedogen* is not readily translatable into English or any other language. 'The term is Dutch, the concept is Dutch, and its application only works in Holland' (website of the philosophy department of Erasmus University in Rotterdam). But this misses the point that penal approaches are highly contested and changeable even within the societies concerned. Despite 'ruling through leniency', Italy has also seen major investigations against political corruption and considerable successes in the fight against the Mafia. And critical reassessment in the Netherlands of the virtues of *gedogen* has clearly affected the possibility of keeping prison rates down – and the desire to do so (Buruma, 2007).

To conclude: this chapter has illustrated some of the challenges in combining both explanatory and interpretative approaches to comparative criminal justice. We have seen that no search for common factors to explain differences in prison rates can do justice to all the differences between individual countries. More qualitative and interpretative approaches, relying on other methods and generating other kinds of data thus provide an essential supplement and corrective to the claims of mainstream work. We have also seen that, if we are to come close to grasping successfully what other systems of criminal justice are actually trying to do, we need to see them 'warts and all'. We should be careful not to deduce intentions from the outcomes being achieved on the basis of what we imagine they *should* be doing – even if these are the best of intentions – and even if it is often tempting – especially for the purposes of advancing a given agenda in local debates – to do just that. As far as Italy is concerned, it can be questioned how far their ways of reducing numbers in prison can rightly be described as expressions of 'inclusion' or tolerance (with the partial exception of the treatment of youth offenders), especially as these 'shields' turn out to be of little help where immigrants are concerned.

FIVE

the challenge of the global

The 'units' that we seek to compare undergo change over time, often as a result of external influences. For some writers, the transformations currently being produced by globalisation go so far as to put into question the comparative project. Katja Aas, author of a superb recent introduction to 'crime and globalisation', argues that 'one can no longer study, for example, Italy by simply looking at what happens inside its territory, but rather need to acknowledge the effects that distant conflicts and developments have on national crime and security concerns and vice versa' (Aas, 2007: 286). Not surprisingly, therefore, she devotes little energy to problems of comparing individual countries, and instead seeks to show us the complex processes by which the 'global' and 'the local' are intertwined. In this chapter I argue that comparative criminal justice must indeed take global and other cross-national interconnections into account, but that it also offers an essential contribution to understanding such developments. I begin by saying more about globalisation and its implications and then focus on case studies of attempts to bring about greater similarities in systems of criminal justice (hence reducing the apparent need for comparison of differences).

Globalisation and comparative criminal justice

Even if we limit ourselves to the narrow question of the implications of globalisation for comparative criminal justice, the literature is overwhelming. Some issues have to do with questions of classification, such as need to define globalisation in relation to related trends such as late-modernity and neo-liberalism, Americanisation or Europe-anization, 'liquid modernity', the move to 'network society' or the rise of the 'risk society'. Others are more descriptive and empirical. What is going on in the various spheres of society and criminal justice that globalisation is said to be affecting? Where are influen-tial norms, scripts, ideas, practices and institutions coming from? Then there are explanatory questions, for example can transna-tional policing be seen as part of the creation a new world order (or rival world orders)? Finally, there are evaluative questions, such as where should ideas be taken from? How much should diversity be respected, why, by whom, and when?

As a consequence of the greater mobility of capital (sometimes but not always embraced as a neo-liberal choice) new forms of interna-tional interconnections grow at the expense of national or more local ones. 'Governance' increasingly replaces government, and power is increasingly shared with other transnational and private actors. Hence many key crime initiatives now link regional or local centres of power (Edwards and Hughes, 2005) or are delegated to the private sector. As it increasingly blurs the differences between 'units', globalisation also reshapes spaces, the meaning of place, and the location and signifi-cance of boundaries. It becomes increasingly difficult to distinguish the 'inside' from the 'outside'. New units emerge as objects and as agents of control. We can think, for example, of the internationalisation of policing (Deflem, 2002) or attempts by international courts of justice to enforce on states common minimal standards of conduct. The same applies to the increasing blurring between war-making, peacekeeping and criminal justice. At the same time, the use of cyberspace requires and generates a variety of forms of control, and may point to new (not necessarily utopian) forms of social ordering.

Comparative criminal justice textbooks and collections are under-standably uncertain about how to integrate such transnational devel-opments into their classificatory and descriptive schemes. Material that fits awkwardly into the traditional comparative paradigm is sometimes relegated to a separate book (Reichel, 2007), to an early chapter (Reichel, 2008), or a closing one (Dammer, Fairchild and Albanese, 2005). Titles such as Winterdyk and Cao's *Lessons from International/Comparative Criminology/Criminal Justice* signal the various topics that are being dealt with, but without saying how, if at all, they may be connected (Winterdyk and Cao, 2004). In their collection, Sheptycki and Wardak have separate sections distinguishing 'area studies', from 'transnational crime issues' and 'transnational control responses' (Sheptycki and Wardak, 2005), but they admit that it is difficult to know when an account of a country's criminal justice system should focus more on internal factors or on external influences. It may be plausible that the chapter on Saudi Arabia treats the country as autonomous, though it also does have a pan-Islamic mission, but it is less obvious why the chapter on South Africa focuses so much on internal developments, whereas the chapter on West Africa is all about its vulnerability to the outside world.

Aas is not the only one who thinks that old-style comparative criminal justice has had its day. In their *Global Criminology and Criminal Justice*, Larsen and Smandych argue that the

> cross-cultural study of crime and justice has evolved from a 'comparative' or 'international' approach to what is now increasingly referred to as a 'transnational' or 'global' approach to crime and justice. ... The effects of rapid globalisation have changed social, political, and legal realities in such a way that comparative and international approaches to crime and justice are inadequate to capture the full complexity of these issues on a global scale.

In particular, they draw attention to 'global trends in policing and security, convergence and divergence in criminal justice and penal policy, and international criminal justice, war crimes and the global protection of human rights' (Larsen and Smandych, 2008: xi). Globalisation has consequences for the economic fortunes of countries, cities, or parts of them, so that ordinary crime problems, and not only those perpetrated by transnational criminal organisations, often have little to do with the unit in which they are located. The same goes for 'solutions' to perceived threats. Aas points out that Norway relies on Italy to keep out unwanted immigrants that might otherwise reach its territory, but it is Italy that then risks international opprobrium in blocking or incarcerating them.

On the other hand, Piers Beirne, in his preface to Larsen and Smandych, warns against going too far. He concedes that globalisation and transnational crime 'blur the relatively distinct boundaries and mobilities that exist between nations and between sovereign territories', but argues that 'comparative criminology still has a vital role to play, both in its own terms and also adjacent to global criminology and as one of its key constituents ... the question of how globalisation and transnational crime affect different societies – similarly or differently, both similarly or differently at the same time, or somewhere in between – is first and foremost a comparative one' (Beirne, 2008: ix). He tells that there is also a valuable role for comparative criminology, for example, in identifying which (failed) states are more vulnerable to the penetration of transnational organised crime – places where there are corrupt politicians, weak controls, lengthy borders, and so on.

The significance of transnational connections can be well illustrated if we revisit the question of explaining why different nation-states have different prison rates. In the last chapter we accepted, for the sake of argument, the distinction between nation-state 'units' presupposed by Cavadino and Dignan. But can we really be sure that what happens in the places they discuss are independent of one other and thus explicable by local economic, social and political factors? Cavadino and Dignan are not unaware of globalisation. They see their findings as proving that differences 'persist' *despite* its effects. But perhaps we then need to say that what they are describing are not so much intrinsic policy differences in the way states choose to deal with marginal citizens *but* differential ways of responding to a similar transnational trend, or even the variable results of the marketing and imitation of an American model of penality.

This alternative perspective complicates any explanation of punitiveness. Neo-liberalism would be seen as an index of the weakening of nation-states. The rise of punitiveness, for example, could reflect attempts by states to reassert their sovereignty, at least as a form of symbolic 'acting-out' (Garland, 1996) or, possibly, as a successful aspect of the restructuring of the regulation of poverty by the neo-liberal penal state (Waquant, 2009a, 2009b). On the other hand, neo-liberalism is not the only transnational trend to affect such rates. The vogue for importing elements of the adversarial process, or for extending more protection to women, can also be relevant. Moreover, southern European countries, which are the places most likely to incarcerate large numbers of immigrants, are not those most influenced by neo-liberalism and its route to a 'new punitiveness' (Solivetti, 2010).

More generally, prison rates need to be seen not only as measures describing the operations of different criminal justice systems – the result of thousands of loosely coordinated local decisions – but also as social artefacts at the centre of wider struggles about changing penal practices. In fact, the adviser to the United Nations, whose figures were the source of Cavadino and Dignan's table, urges all countries, *irrespective of their kind of political economy*, to shape their criminal justice practices so as to aim at a rate of no more than a hundred prisoners per hundred thousand of the population (Walmsley, 1999). (Interestingly, his recommendations of how to reach this goal include avoiding short prison sentences, even though it is the countries with the lowest rates that tend to be the ones that make most use of these.)

Globalisation is just one of the factors leading to the alleged end of the state monopoly over criminal justice (Drake, Muncie and Westmorland, 2010a and b). But it is important to remember that processes of mutual contacts and influence did not start with what is called globalisation. Ideas and practices of criminal justice have always circulated between countries and elites. A previous generation spoke of convergence coming about as a result of the similar technological requirements of industrial societies, and the role of empire and colonialism has also been fundamental in shaping criminal justice systems. Thus, quite apart from the effects of globalisation, the running examples from Italy discussed in this book are only in very limited respects 'intrinsically' Italian. The modern juvenile justice system was initially borrowed from England and Wales (Lemert, 1986). Obligatory prosecution is a practice held in common with some other continental countries, such as Austria, even if it is now an increasingly alien element in a criminal procedure remodelled in Italy in 1989 according to the Anglo-American scheme. Court delays (not in fact a problem in Mussolini's time) have been exacerbated by the introduction of the adversarial procedure because its protections have been added to the previous guarantees for the accused.

None of this borrowing is best described in terms of globalisation. Nor does it prove that comparison should cease to make reference to nation-states. It would be premature to say that the nation-state has had its day as a source of ordering (Loader and Walker, 2007) – all the more so after the economic crisis of 2008 where the market required national states to step in to avoid financial meltdown. Some even see a process of de-globalisation under way. States can also use ostensibly transnational powers for their own local purposes (Sheptycki, 2002). Good comparison will almost always evidence the way nation-states are differently placed in dealing with or being subjected to transnational developments. Countries such as China and Russia are among the better known examples of states that succeed in censoring or manipulating the internet. The same applies to levels of commitment to common standards that are apparently in the interests of all signatories. Within the European Union there are remarkable differences in the way countries implement national or European laws designed to prevent the defrauding the EU budget. In the 1980s the UK pressed strongly for more enforcement, at least until it worried that this could involve ceding sovereignty over criminal law. Italy passed a specific law to deal with this form of criminal behaviour while continuing to rack up the largest frauds (Passas and Nelken, 1993). And nation-states showed little ability to collaborate via European institutions in effectively dealing with the problem (Nelken, 2003b).

It goes without saying, or at least it should do, that globalisation's effects are not easily classified as either 'good' or 'bad' (also because globalisation can communicate the knowledge that can be used to help counteract its bad effects). On a Durkheimian view, where changing forms of social and economic exchange both reflect and produce changing forms of 'moral' interdependence, globalisation could contribute to a new international solidarity, as seen, for example, in the penalising by some countries of sex tourism committed by their citizens abroad, or the strengthening of international criminal justice or the increasing rhetoric of international human rights. In a less utopian spirit, there are certainly many collective problems, from those regarding the environment to financial security, that cannot be solved by states acting alone, as well as many abuses suffered by individuals and groups which cannot safely be left to the states responsible for them to deal with. On the other hand, from a neo-Marxist perspective, globalised exchange can often involve exploitation as businesses and others find ways to avoid criminal penalties in the 'space between the laws' and international bodies impose financial straitjackets in return for loans.

Some writers distinguish between hegemonic or counter-hegemonic globalisation (or between globalisation 'from above' or 'from below') but, in practice, it can be difficult to find fail-safe criteria for picking and choosing what is 'progressive' or not, and we must remember that intentions and outcomes often do not coincide. Any given international blueprint or 'global prescription' (Dezalay and Garth, 2002) can have contradictory effects. The promotion of transparency, as urged by Transparency International, would seem to be an appropriate panacea for corruption, but closer familiarity with the phenomenon in specific contexts shows that transparency also has the effect of entrenching it – the more that is known about the use of underhand methods, the more others may feel they have to do the same (Nelken, 2009a). The attempt to move towards a 'globalising' criminological perspective has the merit of bringing hitherto neglected crimes such as state crimes (including genocide) into better focus (Morrison, 2004). But it can also serve to justify an imaginary 'view from nowhere' that serves mainly to promote Anglo-American models of the criminal justice state that can sap the social control potential of civic society (Newman, 1999; Van Dijk, 2007; cf. Nelken, 2003a). The extension of human rights is a largely positive development, especially for the protection of women and other vulnerable groups (Merry, 2006; Cain and Howe, 2008). But, in the sphere of youth justice, globalisation spreads both an often harsh insistence on greater responsibility as well as a concern to protect rights (Muncie, 2005).

The fight against transnational organised crime offers the best illustration of these points. On the one hand, there are a variety of extremely serious harms committed by such groups. But for almost every one of their activities there are at least two narratives that can be told. One stresses the noble fight of the state and/or relevant non-governmental organisations (e.g. Naim, 2005); the other the extent to which controllers selectively exploit the problems of given victim groups for their own interests (e.g. Van Schendel and Abraham, 2005). The characterisation of organised crime groups often tells us more about political and law enforcement stereotypes than it does about their fluid and changing nature. The repeated scare claim – that criminal justice is territorial whereas organised crime is not confined by national boundaries – tends to exaggerate the degree of collaboration between such groups and to underplay the growth of official responses and the rise of domestic strategies of 'governing through international crime' (Findlay, 2008).

As this suggests, and here comparative criminal justice comes into its own, the local sense of any given global initiative needs to be carefully deconstructed. For example, the Palermo Protocol against human trafficking ('the new slavery' for sexual, child or labour exploitation) has been signed – and ratified – by a very large number of countries. The Protocol has increased the possibility of providing relief to exploited victims of trafficking. But what is at stake in this campaign is not the same for supply, transit and demand countries (or for political elites, employers, workers and others), and the way in which individual countries use the Protocol is shaped by their specific political, cultural and other differences (Munro, 2006). Supply countries have desperate need of the economic remittances of their migrants. Churches in some places in Nigeria pray for the success of those who go abroad so as to earn remittances through some form of prostitution. Among demand countries, Sweden is engaged in an effort to reduce prostitution and makes little or no use of the Palermo Protocol. Germany and the Netherlands are more concerned about having well-regulated systems of sex work.

Italy claims to protect a relatively large number of victims. This may simply be a matter of geography, but another possible reason may be that dealing with prostitutes who decide to ask for help mirrors previous experience in handling ambiguous *pentiti* (the telling term the Italians use to describe Mafia members who agree to collaborate with the authorities). In addition, prosecutors and courts in Italy have a relatively high level of independence from government, whose priority is usually that of limiting immigration. The USA operates sanctions against countries it classifies as being reluctant to stop trafficking, but has learned to live with millions of unregistered Mexican migrants. In the economically advanced (demand) countries, the needs of victims continues to be subordinated to the goal of ending illegal migration. Conversely, some of the victims of even the most atrocious forms of sexual or labour trafficking may prefer their situation to the even worse alternatives left behind (Davies, 2009). It is not easy to do justice in an unjust world (Nelken, forthcoming a).

Making similar? Convergence, copying and collaborating

There is increasing recognition that the globalisation of the 'local' depends on the localisation of the (supposedly) global. But there is still little agreement on how best to study these processes. In his important work on the ways globalisation is affecting youth justice, Muncie distinguishes three of these. The first he calls 'from welfare to neo-liberal governance'. The second he calls 'transfer and convergence' of ideas such as curfews, welfare to work, boot camps and restitutive justice. In a third category he discusses international conventions on the rights of children (Muncie, 2005). But separating out developments into economic, political and legal compartments, while it may be useful for some purposes, also has its limits. The same applies to a recent scheme proposed by Aas that focuses on what she calls 'disembedding, acceleration, movement, standardisation, interconnectedness, vulnerability and re-embedding' (Aas, 2010).

Case studies of the spreading of criminal justice ideas and practices are more promising for this purpose (see e.g. Newburn and Sparks, 2004). But they need to be placed in some larger analytical grid (see Nelken, 2006f) such as one drawing on discussions of transplants and diffusion in the literatures of comparative law and social policy. Thus we can study *what* is being spread – scripts, norms, institutions, technologies, fears, ways of seeing, problems, solutions – new forms of policing, punitiveness, conceptual legal innovations such as the 'the law of the enemy', mediation, restitutive or therapeutic justice. We can also ask from *where to where*, for example from or to national, subnational and supranational levels in Europe, or more widely, or by agreement among signatories to conventions etc., or those subject to regulatory networks, and so on. It takes little skill to discover that what purports to be global frequently comes out of the USA, but members of the European Union, among others, are also quite actively involved, singly and collectively.

We also need to examine *who* is involved. Are the key actors legal ones, such as judges, lawyers, police, probation officers and prison officers (often through meeting colleagues from abroad)? Or are they representatives of businesses, such as security providers or those who build and run private prisons. Or do we have to do with politicians, NGOs or pressure groups, regulatory bodies, journalists, or even academics themselves? Attention needs to be given to the role of institutions, singly, collectively or in competition. In Europe, but also beyond, EU institutions, the Council of Europe and the European Court of Human Rights (EHRC) system are important players. The same crime threat may involve intergovernmental and non-governmental organisations, such as the UN Commissioner for Rights, the International Labour Organisation, or the International Organisation for Migration, Human Rights Watch, Amnesty International, etc.

Another set of questions has to do with *the means* by which criminal justice ideas and practices are being spread. Some exchanges may involve groups of 'experts'; others only concern 'virtual' conversations, as in the way judges read sentences in other jurisdictions as they seek to provide justifications of local practices such as the retention or abolition of the death penalty (Hood, 2001; Macrudden, 2007). Why do various initiatives follow given circuits? How is it that a given practice, such as adversarial justice, can spread so well abroad even while being so much criticised in its home countries? What are the implications of the fact that local agents and institutions often try to use their global influence locally as a source of prestige in competition with other actors. *Why do certain things appeal where they do?* What explains why day fines and conditional dismissals make sense only in some places in Europe? Are there some approaches that everyone wants? Tonry argues that 'technology is a no brainer' and mentions prison security equipment, credit card smart technologies and electronic monitoring (Tonry, 2001). But apparently technical approaches, such as the move to 'actuarial justice' (Feeley and Simon, 1994), can produce quiet revolutions within the field of criminal justice. What counts as 'only' a technical matter will also vary culturally.

Finally, we also need to reflect on *what succeeds and what is meant by success?* Should this be defined in terms of how far it reproduces the original institution or practice or the extent to which an innovation 'fits' into its new place? The Italian penal procedural reform of 1989 has been criticised for having being modified by the higher courts so that it no longer resembles the way it works in the USA (Grande, 2000). But it can be argued that it makes sense to (re)shape the adversarial system in Italy so as to take into account the very real danger of organised crime forcing witnesses to retract their statements at trial. In some cases, borrowing has nothing to do with making the borrower society more like the source of the practice, as for example when economically more developed societies introduce the idea of conflict mediation from less developed ones. In other situations, the aim is to become more like the source of borrowing (and/or the need to be seen to be like them), as with many of the law reforms quickly introduced by many ex-communist countries seeking to be part of the European Union.

Who decides what are the *indicators of 'success'*, and whose claims get to be believed concerning what was supposed to happen – and has happened? Who gets to impose their sense of continuing similarity and difference, and its significance? Can a society get more than it bargained for (Nolan, 2009)? Discussions of the spread of criminal justice ideas and practices sometimes confuse explaining whether a certain model has spread successfully and whether this is a good thing. We are likely to be told that 'zero tolerance' ideas that have not changed practices on the ground are merely 'symbolic' (Jones and Newburn, 2008). On the other hand, if human rights ideas begin to change the local discourse (or add a new layer to it) even if they do not change (other) practices on the ground, this may nonetheless be counted as success (Merry, 2006).

Does the spreading of ideas and practices encouraged by globalisation reduce differences among systems of criminal justice? To examine this key question it can be useful to distinguish among processes of convergence, copying and collaborating. Convergence can produce more similarities even where this is not the aim. Copying, by contrast, is an example of actively seeking similarity through borrowing or imitation. Collaborating, finally, involves trying to understand what others are doing so as to facilitate coordinated action, even if we do not necessarily want to copy them.

Convergence has both objective and subjective aspects. Although technological and other changes can reflect and produce the need for similarity, it is also important to see (contrary to much writing on the subject) that globalisation and homogenisation do not always go together (Nelken, 1997c). In its economic aspects, globalisation relies on and often reproduces economic and social *differentiation*. And neo-liberalism too is compatible with socio-cultural differences between places (these can even be marketed). Cyberspace has lent itself not only to efforts to transcend boundaries of place and tradition, but is also used by those who seek to create tightly-bounded groups united by hate of those with different identities (Roversi, 2008). At the subjective level, the spread of globalising common sense means that distant forces penetrate local worlds and that local meanings are often dislodged (Coombe, 1998). People in Germany fed on television episodes of Perry Mason assumed that they too had an adversarial system of criminal justice. Conversely, Garland's work on *the culture of control* was soon translated and used by left-leaning Italians scholars as a spur to resisting the local tightening of official social control interpreted as essentially part of the same process (even if, arguably, this had more to do with the response to immigration). As this reminds us, the 'same' ideas in different contexts are not necessarily the same – and do not have the same effects.

When we study processes of borrowing and imitation we again discover that social actions do not always have the consequences that are sought. Jones and Newburn examined the outcomes of efforts in England and Wales to introduce US practices regarding private prisons, 'three strikes and you're out' sentencing reform, and zero tolerance policing. The authors saw themselves as trying to reconcile 'insights coming from the broad global convergence and local divergence vantage points' (Jones and Newburn, 2008: 8). Although they found clear evidence of borrowing taking place, they concluded that this has made relatively little difference in practice. By contrast, another recent description of transplanting US-style institutions (that unfortunately does not refer to Jones and Newburn) comes to somewhat different conclusions. In his excellent account of the introduction of US-type problem-solving courts to five other common law jurisdictions, Nolan stresses how much was successfully taken over. His concern, if anything, is that such borrowing will eventually bring about some penetration of wider aspects of US culture in societies that are purportedly somewhat critical of it (Nolan, 2009).

These authors may be using different criteria for judging 'success'. Newburn and Jones are worried that borrowing from the USA could increase incarceration rates (and their negative finding help explain the continuing gulf between the USA and England and Wales). Nolan has a more diffuse fear of cultural imperialism. He also recognises that any borrowing is inevitably affected by differences in the legal and general culture of the importing country. Indeed, he shows us how the actors involved explicitly sought to modify what they were importing. Both Nolan and Jones and Newburn restricted themselves to borrowing among jurisdictions within the common law world. Interestingly, however, Waquant is convinced that American cultural assumptions about crime have easily penetrated thinking in Continental European countries such as France (Waquant, 2009a, 2009b).

Many studies of collaboration in criminal justice worry about who is in charge and where it may lead. But they spend less time in discussing how it is even possible. Jacqueline Ross argues that champions of closer transnational cooperation may be too quick to envision it occurring through a series of technical fixes. In a series of richly detailed analyses she shows the considerable theoretical difficulties faced by those she interviewed when seeking to bring their own working practices into alignment with those that belong to other systems of criminal justice (e.g. Ross, 2004, 2007). In particular, she focuses on the significance for cooperating in the battle against transnational crime of the fact that the USA and European nations conceptualise, legitimate and control undercover policing in substantially dissimilar ways.

Ross tells us that covert operations are everywhere controversial but that this may not always be for the same reason. In comparing American and Italian ways of formulating the issue, she argues that whereas Americans primarily worry that covert agents may corrupt innocent targets, Italians are especially concerned that covert operations may slide into state-sanctioned lawlessness (Ross, 2004). In America effort is made to strengthen the rights of the potential object of entrapment, but in Italy it is left to the prosecutor to keep the police in line. There are also considerable differences in the status given to informants and what they are allowed to do by way of breaking the law. Ross doubts that harmonisation of these countries' legal regimes is feasible, even if this type of law enforcement is treated as exceptional and given its own special rules. She concludes with a mental experiment that shows that there would be need to be a major change in the domestic roles of prosecutors for the two countries to be able to work properly together (Ross, 2004: 306). The extent of remaining differences is all the more remarkable given that Italy is the Continental European country that has done most to try to move towards the adversarial system.

Not the least of the differences that Ross underlines is her recognition that giving Italian prosecutors discretion not to enforce the law would involve changing the constitution. As we have seen when discussing obligatory prosecution, the second of our running examples, the stumbling block for many Italians is the danger that recognising the need for discretion can easily allow the government of the day to set and change priorities according to its own interests. She also notes that it is hard for outsiders to understand or copy the Italian way of unofficial official discretion which allows them to work around rules where officially there is no discretion. As she rightly says, this puts a premium on being able to cover your back through political and personal networks (but she does not mention that this is true in Italy more generally). Ross also tells us about other practical problems that obstruct cooperation, from the lack of legal status for US undercover agents in Italy, to the lack of the language skills that would allow Italians to penetrate foreign crime rings. Yet it is also important to remember that the media also report many examples of 'successful ' collaboration, for example in apprehending suspected terrorists (even if not always on equal terms). This may be because Italy's secret service(s) quite often do not keep to their own laws, and the police often respond to political dictates before later (sometimes much later) being brought to book by the more proactive members of the judiciary.

As this implies, in addition to the many descriptive, explanatory and interpretative issues raised by the cross-national spread of criminal justice ideas and practices, there are also value questions of what this spreading does, could do or should do to diversity. Increasingly, the question of diversity between cultures overlaps with that of respecting diversity within a society. If units are less and less distinguishable, this is in part also because of population movements. The many young female judges in the Italian courts increasingly find themselves processing young Muslim offenders, usually by fast-track procedures for those caught *en flagrente*. On the wall hangs a crucifix. The legend inscribed over the bench reads that 'the law is equal for all'. But this may not be the way it is perceived. What aspects of this everyday situation, if any, should be treated as requiring more respect for diversity? More generally, as diasporic communities grow larger and more confident, the question arises to what extent nation-states should explicitly delegate to them powers of conflict-processing.

International human rights standards are hammered out over years of negotiation so as to find phrasings that satisfy representatives of different countries and NGOs. But diversity re-emerges in the way such agreements are implemented. Although there is some debate about the possibility and merits of harmonising private law (especially within the European Union), discussion of this key question in the area of criminal law has been slower in coming. For a long time – even within the sphere of the European Union – politicians defended the distinctive features of their criminal law procedures, and only a few academics argued for a more common approach. More recently, there has been a change of heart, largely attributable to the threat of transnational crimes, especially terrorism, as well as concerns over irregular immigration. Within the European Union there has been some progress in creating shared policing and prosecuting institutions – and not only where this helps protect the European Union's own funds. The European Court of Human Rights strives to arrive at some minimal standards in penal procedures, prisoners' rights and similar matters.

But even what seem the most obvious attempts to improve procedural protections for all defendants can be shown to often make mistaken assumptions about how different legal cultures operate and need to operate. Standards drawn from the adversarial form of trial can be based on a misreading of the logic of continental systems (Lasser, 2005), just as continentals often conflate the common law with its American expression. More generally, should we see reduction of diversity, in so far as it can be achieved, as progress or as a problem? So much of course depends on what is at issue – the decline in use of the death penalty, the elimination of torture, the setting of minimal standards for prisoners? Or are we speaking of sharing common definitions of corruption or ideas of how criminal procedures should be organised?

The author of a recent introduction to comparative criminal justice offers the following reflections by way of conclusion to his book. 'Globalisation' he says, 'will diminish the variety of criminal justice systems. Common threats will invite common responses, which will increase the similarities in criminal justice systems around the world'. He goes on to say that 'on the one hand, this could be seen as a loss'. But, on the other hand, 'criminal justice systems are not like the natural world, where we should celebrate diversity for its own sake. Increased requirements for communication and harmonisation provide rewards for convergence, and criminal justice systems will, after all, be judged on their effectiveness' In any case, he concludes, 'one can remain sure that as long as cultures, languages, public opinions and social discourses differ, so will criminal justice systems and the way they operate' (Pakes, 2004: 178).

These remarks, thoughtful as they are, also beg a number of questions. Is there really no reason to value diversity for its own sake once we recognise that criminal justice systems are not part of the natural world? What of the benefits of maintaining a variety of forms of social experimentation? What of the need for procedure to fit society's values and its traditions? What if the greater homogeneity that emerges through the imitation or imposition of a currently successful Anglo-American model reflects and produces the sort of society that requires a high level of punishment? Familiarity with the differences among criminal justice systems, including the three running examples from Italy that I have been using, should also make us cautious about the claim that systems of criminal justice 'after all will be judged on their effectiveness'. Who will be (who should be?) the judge of effectiveness? It is not enough to say that 'the balance between fairness and effectiveness' will be worked out differently in different places. The issue is rather whether what these terms mean stays the same and how far the metaphor of 'balancing' these 'values' is shared cross-culturally.

Whether or not the source is rightly described as globalisation, pressures for conformity do seem to be rising (Nelken, 2006f). But there can often be confusion between what is normal in the sense of not falling below a standard and in the somewhat different meaning of what is normal or average. Take again one of my running examples. It is important to ask how far the Strasbourg Court of Human Rights is imposing 'universal' principles of good practice of criminal procedure on the signatories to the convention it enforces, and how far – as in imposing limits on acceptable court delays – it is (also) involved in a process of 'normalisation' to a European average (Nelken, 2004a, 2008).

Why are trials that are too short – in the sense that they are well below the average time devoted to trial in comparable places – not also considered a breach of human rights? Is it right to threaten Italy with exclusion from the European Convention on Human Rights for conduct which follows from the fact that is an outlier? The only other signatory treated in this way is Turkey, for its failure to comply over Cyprus and its continuing maltreatment of the Kurds. Italian court times do create suffering. Justice delayed is, too often, justice denied. But it is at least questionable whether excessive court delay is the same sort of breach of human rights as torture.

SIX

whose sense?

In this final chapter, by way of conclusion, I discuss in turn the place of knowledge, understanding and method in comparative criminal justice and the role of researchers in constructing discourses about other peoples' systems of criminal justice. After describing some of the traps lying in wait for those who blindly rely on local 'experts', I consider how far these can be avoided using the three research methods I call 'virtual comparison', 'researching there', and 'living there'.

On knowledge

We have seen in the previous chapters that criminal justice is not just a set of actions to be described, but is part of broader cultural ways of thinking, as found in a variety of locations or sites of interpretation. To appreciate other ways of defining and delivering official sanctions cannot just be a matter of identifying different units (states, organisations, professional work groups or whatever) which exhibit varying practices and procedures. We also need to deal with the different logics that structure what is known (and what it is thought possible and desirable to know). For example, does the criminological distinction between 'white-collar' and 'organised' crime correspond to an ontological reality? Or does it reflect a Protestant conception of the ethics of wealth production that presupposes the inherent respectability of moneymaking and the ethnic composition of organised crime (Ruggiero, 1996)?

There are important contrasts in national criminological literatures regarding what crimes are thought most worthy of attention, and which actors in the system are authorised to deal with them. There may also be telling differences in the availability and use of empirical descriptions of the work of police or other criminal justice actors. On the other hand, both mainstream and critical discourses (Van Swaaningen, 1997) also cross-cut national boundaries. While discourses such as rehabilitation or just deserts may have origins in particular places, their adoption hardly ever stops at the boundaries of national jurisdictions. The same applies to current attempts to introduce, monitor or regulate international standards. Ways of thinking are shared by various intellectual and policy networks (Edwards and Hughes, 2005) or 'transnational epistemic communities' (Karstedt, 2002). Scholarly criminological discourse in turn is part of (and has varying influence on) a larger series of purported knowledges, ranging from that found in official documents, through media and internet journalism, to popular culture and even advertisements, all of which help mould ideas about crime and its control.

Both explanatory and interpretative approaches can be brought to bear on the question how knowledge is produced and used. We can ask, for example, about the causes and effects of such 'knowledge'. Can American ideas about crime spread without necessarily leading to a rise in incarceration rates? What consequences are produced by classifications of levels of judicial integrity or rates of incarceration? How far does the publication of the results of public opinion surveys about fear of crime or attitudes to the criminal justice system make them self-fulfilling? Vagaries in what is considered 'knowledge', or who is considered an expert, can itself be a factor in accounting for changes in criminal justice, as seen in the growth of prestige of economists, accountants and experts in risk evaluation in the USA and the UK. But these developments may take a different form in different places, depending (as between the USA, Germany and Poland) on the classes whose ideas are hegemonic, the role of bureaucracies and competition between media outlets (Savelsberg, 1994, 1999; Savelsberg, King and Cleveland, 2002).

On the other hand, making sense of what passes for knowledge also involves questions of meaning. The scientific literature is often less culturally universal than it purports to be. Much influential criminal justice literature is American and carries entrenched culturally-specific assumptions about the nature of crime and the role of criminal justice. It takes for granted the modern Anglo-American 'pragmatic instrumental' approach with its supposed aim of reducing recidivism. While insisting on getting beyond myths, it fails to see why, in some places, and at some times in all places, words speak louder than actions. Understanding criminal justice in an interpretative vein involves attempting to grasp the meaning of what other people are actually trying to do. But we also have to take into account the possibility that actors are not fully aware of what they are doing – and, still less, of its consequences.

The complexities of interpreting can be made clearer by taking as an example some remarks by Massimo Pavarini, a leading Italian criminologist. In an English-language article, he set out to explain what he saw as the implications of the ordinary Italian's rejection of the state, and of the absence of Protestant structures of responsibility. 'Its raining ... damn the government', he says, 'very aptly sums up how an abstract, impersonal entity is blamed for everything that is seen as socially evil, unjust, undesirable and frightening. The Italian political lexicon is a complex weave of two historic traditions: the catholic matrix with its providential conception of history in which universal judgement has always outweighed individual judgement, and the Marxist matrix with its belief in the rebirth of society through revolution. Both these cultural traditions have encouraged the process whereby social expectations do not entail individual responsibility for society's ills' (Pavarini, 1997: 95).

A number of issues arise. How is this account likely to be understood by those with no first-hand experience of Italy? What does it mean to say that social expectations do not entail individual responsibility? In my experience of everyday life I see a rich texture of intertwined social and individual demands and expectations. So is this account to be read more as a critical 'intervention' by an engaged participant, and less as an effort at disinterested description? (Is it relevant that this statement is being made by a leading (ex)-Marxist criminologist in a book edited by a (once?) Marxist scholar? And what of the fact that Pavarini is himself personally one of the most responsible people one could ever hope to meet?) Even the most well informed of Italian criminologists, then, provides us with an interpretation of his society in the form of a riddle. Whatever else they show, these remarks also offer, albeit unwittingly, further proof of the extent to which Italians are unusually inclined to speak badly of their own society. During 2008 there was a news report of a German offender who managed to get himself smuggled home from prison by using the post office to mail himself there in a large package. The Italian media commented that in Italy he might have made it out of prison but he would never have arrived home!

On understanding

If even experts need to be interpreted, this makes it all the more important to consider *which* informants we treat as experts and why we think they can be trusted. Yet most researchers are reluctant to recognise the implications of the fact that, in all cultures, descriptions and criticisms of social and legal ideas and practices carry, and are intended to carry, political implications. When we think of experts in own culture we will often, without much difficulty, be able to associate them with 'standing' for given political or policy positions. But it is no less essential, if more difficult, to be aware of this factor when we rely on informants from abroad. Think of the problem of deciding how far Italian judges involved in fierce battles with government proposals are mainly concerned with defending themselves as a corporation. Some politicians, practitioners and academics are notoriously pro-judges, while others are virulently against them. The same applies to Italian criminologists writing about immigration and crime. There are bitter disputes over the question whether illegal and unregulated immigrants are over-represented in criminal activity because they commit more crime, or are victims of selective criminalisation and the social constructions of (only certain) aspects of the crime problem. Whom do outsiders decide to believe and how do they decide? If there is any type of criminology in which 'reflexivity' (Nelken, 1994a) is of the essence, it is surely comparative criminology. But it is unusual for researchers to include discussions of the way they are themselves *part* of the context they are describing (Nelken, 2007c).

The issue 'whom can you trust?' is therefore as relevant to the process of doing research as it is to understanding criminal behaviour and responses to it (Nelken, 1994b). Who is 'authorised' to speak for a given legal system or specific practice? How do their roles, as politicians or policy-makers, members of the system, judges or other regulators of the system, employees of NGOs or pressure groups, journalists, academics or whatever, influence their knowledge and accounts of the systems they are describing. In the UK, police spokespersons provide influential accounts of the crime problem and individual criminals; this is much less true in Italy. On the other hand, in Italy, judges and prosecutors are perhaps the major sources of information about organised crime. Their 'motivations' of judicial sentences sometime run to thousands of circumstantially documented pages and few people worry about the dangers of using evidence crafted for legal purposes as if it were a sociological treatise.

Why should informants tell us what they know? Each criminal justice organisation is likely to have an 'official line' that it wishes to promote and secrets that it wants to conceal. Some informants may tell us openly that the position they are taking is an unconventional or personal one that is not shared by others. But, more often, they will want us to credit their view as the only one possible. 'Correct' answers by police in Japan, Johnson tells us, reflect *tatamae*, or socially approved image management (Johnson, 2003: 141). But is this not also true for Japanese prosecutors? And is this problem only relevant in Japan? Can we be more certain of our findings if informants coming from different groups provide the same accounts? Take the question of similarities and differences between what academics and practitioners have to say. If academics and practitioners agree, could this be only because the academics are relying uncritically on information from the practitioners? If they disagree, could this be because academics are too cut off from what actually goes on?

Even when we are sure that our sources are not 'partial' to one side or another – or we try to make allowance for this – there still remains the problem that experts and practitioners are undoubtedly part of their own culture. This is, after all, why we consult them. But this means that it is easy to fall into a comedy of errors in which we look for what is of interest to us, and they tell us what they think we want to know even if it is not what we should want to know. If we set out to understand why in the USA or UK criminal justice is relatively harsh we are less likely to find informants working in the system who share this preoccupation than people worried that not enough is being done to protect the public from crime – and this explains, in part, why the system is relatively severe. If we are interested in explaining why Italian juvenile justice is so tolerant

(Nelken, 2006b, 2006c), our informants are more likely to be on the look out for signs of harshness – indeed it is precisely that vigilance which helps explains the leniency of the system. In England and Wales, a system highly influenced by managerial considerations will be criticised for its inefficiencies. In Italy, a principled but inefficient system will regularly be attacked by local commentators on grounds of principle.

Cavadino and Dignan (2006b) make use of a series of academic informants so as to fill in the details of what they call the 'idiosyncrasies' of the societies they are comparing. But they tell us very little about how they chose their collaborators, nor seem to be aware that each will have his or her own disciplinary biases and local political allegiances. As far as Italy is concerned they rely mainly on a legal scholar who is a well known expert on juvenile justice, whilst also making extensive reference to the now somewhat dated writings of the early 1990s by Pavarini, a very different kind of criminologist, whose larger claims – as we have seen – can also sometimes be challenging to interpret. And *mutanda mutandis* the same applies to the other countries they discuss.

On method

From what has been said so far about the difficulties of interpreting another society's practices, it should be clear that the method we adopt to overcome such obstacles will have crucial effects on the substance of our findings. Whether we are doing, reading or using comparative research, we must be aware that claims about why things take the form they do can never be separated from the issue of *how* sense is made of them – and *whose* sense that is. The three possible strategies I have elsewhere described as 'virtually there', researching there', and 'living there' (Nelken, 2000a) may help to clarify what is involved in cooperating with foreign experts in other places, in interviewing legal officials and others in their own contexts, and in drawing on direct experience of living and working in the country concerned.

The approach called 'virtually there' uses cross-cultural collaboration as its means of arriving at reliable accounts of relevant differences between systems of criminal justice. Instead of going to learn about a foreign culture at first hand, the researcher is content to be 'virtually there', by relying on an inside expert from the society or societies. At its worst, this can be a fig leaf for the worst sort of 'comparison by juxtaposition'. But, at its best, experts in the distinctive traditions of the societies in which they live and work take on the task of educating experts in the other system. Each therefore tries to familiarise the other with salient aspects of their own system in terms that can be related back to aspects of the other society. Such collaboration requires a high degree of mutual trust and often involves 'negotiating' mutually acceptable descriptions of legal practice in each of their home countries.

An excellent example of what can be achieved in this way is found in Brants and Field's comparison of controversial aspects of police practice in England and Wales as compared to the Netherlands (Brants and Field, 2000). Among other insights, they noted that in England and Wales, diversion was seen as a somewhat 'guilty secret', which compromised the ideals of adversarial justice in the interests of making the criminal process more expeditious. Diversion in the Netherlands, by contrast, was understood as an aspect of the wider 'politics of accommodation', which encouraged an ample use of prosecution and other official discretion. They also contrasted the changing 'demons' that were used to justify undercover police practices in the countries compared.

'Researching there', by contrast, is an approach in which the researcher is in direct contact with informants in their own society. This method can be illustrated by David Johnson's interviewing a large number of prosecutors in Japan so as to explain differences in 'role expectations' there as compared to the USA (Johnson, 2000). Johnson's main interest was in understanding why prosecutors in Japan so often go out of their way not to charge suspects. Prosecution aims that are at home in Anglo-American legal cultures, such as that of 'disposing efficiently of as many cases as possible', came low down the list for the Japanese. The most important goals to which they subscribed turned out to be that of 'discovering the truth' and 'making the correct decision whether to charge with an offence'. Interestingly, low priority was also given to the objective of 'invoking public condemnation of the crime', considered important by less than a third of his sample. Many of those interviewed did not even understand what this meant. Rather than seeking to clarify cultural assumptions through collaboration with other experts, or by attempting to move backwards and forward between his own culture and that under observation, Johnson's interview schedule was carefully designed to produce the same stimulus for all respondents so as to be able to standardise their answers. However, he admits that his approach has limits that need to be set against its strengths. For example, the questions Johnson planned to ask about whether prosecutors *actually achieved* their objectives were ruled off-limits.

The third approach, which I have dubbed 'living there', involves wider participation in the general life of the country and may even include an active consulting/critical role in relation to the criminal justice system itself. The scholars who use this approach can be described as 'observing participants' (rather than participant observers) who come to enjoy the status of 'insider-outsiders' (Nelken, 2004b). Maureen Cain, for example, spent a total of eight years in the West Indies before returning to Britain, and she was able to draw directly on her own experience of teaching and action rather than limiting herself to retelling what professionals or experts had to say (Cain, 2000a, 2000b). She tells us, for example, that the students she taught wanted what they considered to be accredited 'universal' knowledge but that she felt ill at ease:

> Teaching about youth cultures in society which is not rigidly age stratified; of teaching community policing and democratic accountability while lacking a language to describe a post-colonial service lacking a sense of direction, having lost its *raison d'être*, of talking ethnic minorities where historically – and arguably today as well – it is the culture and identity of the black former *majority* which is under threat. (Cain, 2000a: 265)

Different research strategies have different merits and there are the usual trade-offs, such as being able to cover more cases with questionnaires or interviews as opposed to in-depth observation, and so on. Methods can only be judged in terms of the objectives being pursued and it is important to appreciate that each operate under their own constraints. The choice to follow any particular approach to data gathering in comparative research will be linked to the many considerations which influence the feasibility of a given research project, including the time available, and whether one is able to visit the country concerned. But the three methods distinguished here can be placed on a continuum running from least to greatest engagement with another society, and this has a number of implications. Virtual research and short research visits, by their nature, can require too much reliance on local experts and practitioners. Long-term involvement in a culture, by contrast, makes it more possible to discover the intellectual and political affiliations of our informants and gain direct experience of the relationship between criminal justice and wider aspects of the same society.

Actually living in a place for a long period is the best – perhaps the only reliable – way to get a sense of what is salient. Seeing the difficulties of keeping to the many over rigid legal rules in Italy gives you more idea of why some people avoid them, and of what the judges are up against in their attempts to enforce them. Seeing how social control is exercised in Italian family life is indispensable for understanding what is and is not asked of its juvenile justice system. Having a social and occupation role in italian life was also helpful for finding out more about the practices that I have been using as running examples. I gained a deeper understanding of the actual effects of the rule of obligatory prosecution when a family friend explained that she would have liked to reserve her energies for pollution cases rather than low-level infractions without social consequences, but that her boss had threatened her with disciplinary proceedings if she risked allowing unimportant cases to fall into prescription. Participating in a national law professors' project on legal delay made it easier to appreciate how far lengthy trials were the desired or undesired outcomes of procedural complexities.

A further advantage of actually living in a country comes from being better placed to convey in a convincing way the experience of what Geertz calls 'being there' (Geertz, 1988). Whether this be seen as some sort of reaction to the otherwise paralysing postmodern 'crisis of representation', or, more straightforwardly, as a way of dealing with the suspicion that one has not really got to grips with the culture being (re)presented, there is no doubt that the descriptions that most influence an audience often take the form of vignettes drawn from life. The more opportunities to do this, the more convincing the argument as the story *of* the research comes to join the stories *in* the research.

But we should not exaggerate the differences between adopting one or other of these methodologies. The insider-outsider's direct 'experience' is always and necessarily marked by expectations based on previous socialisation – and the difficult trick is that of losing one type of ethnocentrism without taking on another. Because the observing participant can experience directly only a small slice of life she, like those who use the other methodological approaches, is still largely reliant on other people for ideas and information which lie beyond her direct experience. A person who lives in a place can also no longer pretend to the same useful naiveté of a visitor. Once they have a recognized internal identity those with other loyalties will also be less willing to trust them (and they will compete for the same scarce resources.)

The insider-outsider too must learn from and contribute to a wider 'scientific' literature. But, on the other hand, direct experience can help in grasping the meaning of concepts such as 'clientalism' in a way that a mere literature search can never do. It is quite different, for example, actually encountering (and perhaps suffering) one version of this intricate combination of instrumental friendship and sponsored co-optation and then going back to the scientific literature to learn more about the wider varieties of this form of social and political ordering. The insider-outsider is also often in a good position to appreciate how given literatures which present themselves as standing above partial perspectives are in fact shaped by scholars with specific roles and standpoints.

Frances Heidensohn, an insightful writer on comparative issues, has recently proposed a richer classification than the three methods described above. She argues that it can be helpful to distinguish among accounts coming from strangers, refugees, explorers, reformers, bureaucrats, armchair travellers and global theorists (Heidensohn, 2006, 2007). These categories can be especially helpful, she suggests, in showing how different roles can contribute to a division of labour of comparative work. Data, she argues, is typically provided by bureaucrats and explorers, concepts come from strangers (but also from armchair and global theorists), whereas frameworks come from travellers of both types who gain overviews from their real or virtual journeys.

The three approaches I set out were not intended to cover all aspects of conceiving and executing comparative research projects. But it is hard to see how or why the division of labour Heidensohn describes would actually come about between actors with such different reasons for seeking to understand criminal justice practices. On the other hand, often the same researchers switch between, or combine, the various roles that she outlines. For example, academics are currently collaborating with the NGO Transparency International under a Seventh Framework programme of the European Commission with the aim of designing better anti-corruption tools under the title of 'Promotion of Participation and Citizenship in Europe through the Advocacy and Legal Advice Centres of Transparency International: Analysis and Enhancement of an Anti-corruption Tool to Enable Better Informed and Effective Citizen Participation in Europe'.

Another, not untypical collaborative project under the auspices of JUSTIS calls on the talents of a number of European criminologists in a pioneering cross-national study of prosecution. This, we are told, 'is a project designed to provide EU institutions and Member States with new evidence-based indicators of public trust in justice'. The aim of the project is to develop and pilot survey-based indicators with the stated intention being not only to understand common features and important differences, but also to view these in the context of the planned common legal space within the EU and the tentative plans for a supra-national prosecution service. The project's interim findings supply lots of useful information about the systems being compared, often with the help of flow charts, special attention being given to what happens at each stage of the process in different jurisdictions. On the other hand, the goal of achieving more through disposals of high-volume crime is simply taken for granted. No mention is made, for example, in reference to Italy, of the role of obligatory prosecution and other specific features of the Italian legal system, nothing is said about the context of ongoing struggles between prosecutors and politicians, nor is any thought given to the political implications that proposals for standardisation with other places might have for this or similar issues in Italy or elsewhere. The issues that matter are taken to be legal, technical and managerial ones. This is not to say, however that there is any necessary contradiction between practical engagement and valid research. The European Committee on Torture, for example, is one of the few sources of essential data on the international treatment of vulnerable people by different police forces and prison authorities (Morgan, 2000).

We need to be careful not to confuse ways of getting data with the use that will be made of it. In particular, the time spent in a place tells you little about what conclusions are likely to be drawn. For example, Clinard's short visit to Switzerland led him to a positive assessment of the country's way with crime (Clinard, 1978), but Balvig's even shorter visit there led him to more critical conclusions (Balvig, 1988). On the other hand, Downes (1988) needed only a short period to be impressed with prison policy in the Netherlands whereas his Dutch critics, actually living there, were much more cynical (Franke, 1990). On the basis of relatively short periods of research, Crawford criticises King, who lived for some years in France, for failing to see the downside of the French approach to crime prevention (Crawford, 2000b). What can be relevant to at least some of these disagreements is whether the study of foreign cultures is actually more about the home country than the setting being studied. It is reasonable to suppose that, as a very general rule, an insider-outsider who spends a long time in a foreign country is likely to become less interested in examining it for the lessons it supposedly has to teach those back home (except when writing for an audience in their country of origin) and as much, or more, in trying to understand it in relation to its own history and current challenges. They may also, by choice or otherwise, embrace a general world view closer to the new place where they are located (Bond, 1997).

The insider-outsider, whose work is not constrained by cross national policy-oriented projects or plans for harmonisation, may be asked or tempted to take part in the national or local debates and conflicts of her new society. In my own case, as an Anglo-American criminologist transplanted to Italy during the *Tangentopoli* anti-corruption investigations, it mattered to insiders whether I was 'for' or 'against' the judges. After writing some articles about *Tangentopoli* for English-speaking readers, I wrote a chapter in Italian, in a collection for a respected series of volumes on Italian history, that attempted to tell the story of what had happened (Nelken, 1997b). I thought the piece was favourable to what the judges had achieved, and some senior left-wing judges later recommended it to their readers. But because it did also contain some mild criticisms it was also seized on by writers sympathetic to the politicians under attack and praised in Parliament by a notoriously anti-judge deputy. I was then invited to act as an expert witness by lawyers defending a businessman facing extradition from the USA for what seemed then like a serious case of corruption. My task would have been to explain to the American courts that the crimes uncovered by *Tangentopoli* should have been considered political offences (Nelken, 2002). I declined this invitation, the businessman was in fact extradited, but the court then found the facts he was accused of not to exist.

Political corruption in Italy is no longer at the centre of local criminal justice debates, though it never seems to disappear for long. The burning issue now concerns the relationship between immigration and crime and the way this has encouraged fear of street crime. Should this new concern about crime be understood (and opposed) as further evidence of the spread of American, hegemonic, neo-liberal-inspired ideas of punitiveness, as many left-leaning criminologists would have it? Or should it (also) be seen as a sign of a more democratic, bottom-up growth in individualist, consumer-based approach to politics and law that in Italy is accompanying the inevitable (?) decline of (solidaristic) ideologies. Insider-outsiders have to relate their opinions and observations on this and other questions to those of the native members of the culture with whom they interact. They may take themselves serving as a translator, commentator or counterpoint in respect to the views of their informants. Sometimes they will find the conformity of their colleagues or other informants judgements with their own views as evidence for the soundness of their observations, at other times they may see more value in the freshness of the outsider's perspective and see what natives say as data that itself needs interpretation.

Whatever choice is made, the methods we choose and the way we use them are not only a means to obtaining information but are also intimately linked to the substance of what we find or think we find. They are an essential part of the ethical and political reasons for doing comparative work (Roberts, 2002), involving as this does engaging with and 'representing' the other, and being open to being changed by such encounters. It may be true that keeping faith with others' meanings may not always be the only value in play. We may sometimes need to impose common meanings in order to get a collaborative project off the ground (Klockars, Ivkovich and Haberfeld, 2004). In some circumstances, depending on our approach to social science, we may even think that we know better than the people we are studying, the meaning of what they are doing – or its implications. Or our goal may simply be to try and change what they are doing. But in all such cases, at the least we should be mindful of what is involved in making sense of difference – and conscious of the dangers of our presumption.

references

Aas, Katja, F. (2007) *Globalisation and Crime*. London: Sage.

Aas, Katja, F. (2010) 'Victimhood of the national? Denationalizing sovereignty in crime control', in Adam Crawford (ed.), *International and Comparative Criminal Justice and Urban Governance*. Cambridge: Cambridge University Press.

Aebi, Marcello F. and Stadnic, Nina (2007) *Council of Europe Annual Penal Statistics*, SPACE I, 2005 survey on prison populations. Strasbourg: Council of Europe.

Balvig, Flemming (1988) *The Snow-white Image: The Hidden Reality of Crime in Switzerland,* Scandinavian Studies in Criminology. Oslo: Norwegian University Press.

Baruma, Ian (2006) *Murder in Amsterdam: The Death of Theo Van Gogh and the Limits of Tolerance*. Harmondsworth: Penguin.

Becker, Howard, S. (1997) *Tricks of the Trade.* Chicago: Chicago University Press.

Beckett, Katherine (1997) *Making Crime Pay: The Politics of Law and Order in the Contemporary United States*. New York: Oxford University Press.

Beirne, Piers (1983/1997) 'Cultural relativism and comparative criminology', reprinted in Piers Beirne and David Nelken (eds), *Issues in Comparative Criminology*. Aldershot: Dartmouth. pp. 3–24.

Beirne, Piers (2008) 'Preface', in Nick Larsen and Russell Smandych (eds), *Global Criminology and Criminal Justice: Current Issues and Perspectives*. Buffalo, NY: Broadview Press. p. xi.

Birkbeck, Christopher and Pérez-Santiago, Neelie (2006) 'The character of penal control in Latin America: sentence remissions in a Venezuelan prison', *Criminology and Criminal Justice*, 6 (3): 289–308.

Birkbeck, Christopher (forthcoming) 'Imprisonment and internment: comparing penal institutions North and South', in Charles Wood (ed.), *Crime, Law and Governance in the Americas*. Santiago Chile: Editorial Catalonia. pp. 133–60.

Black, Donald (1976) *The Behaviour of Law*. New York: Academic Press.

Body-Genrot, Sophie (2000) *The Social Control of Cities? A Comparative Perspective*. Oxford: Blackwell.

Bond, Michael H. (1997) 'Two decades of chasing the dragon: a Canadian psychologist assesses his career in Hong Kong', in Michael H. Bond (ed.), *Working at the Interface of Cultures: Eighteen Lives in Social Science*. London: Routledge. p. 172.

Braithwaite, John (1989) *Crime, Shame and Re-integration*. Cambridge: Cambridge University Press.

Brants, Chrisje (2011) 'Comparing criminal process as part of legal culture', in David Nelken (ed.), *Comparative Criminal Justice and Globalisation*. Aldershot: Ashgate.

Brants, Chrisje and Field, Stewart (2010) 'Legal culture, political cultures and procedural traditions: towards a comparative interpretation of covert and proactive policing in England and Wales and the Netherlands', in David Nelken (ed.), *Contrasting Criminal Justice*. Aldershot: Dartmouth. pp. 77–116.

Brown, David (2005) 'Continuity, rupture or just more of the volatile and contradictory', in John Pratt et al. (eds), *The New Punitiveness*. Cullompton: Willan Publishing. p. 27.

Brownlie, Ian (1998) 'New labour, new penology: punitive rhetoric and the limits of managerialism in criminal justice policy', *Journal of Law and Society*, 25: 313–35.

Buruma, Ybo (2007) 'Dutch tolerance: on drugs, prostitution and euthenasia', in Michael Tonry and Catriene Bijleveld (eds), *Crime and Justice in the Netherlands*. Chicago: Chicago University Press. pp. 73–113.

Cain, Maureen (2000a) 'Through other eyes: on the limitations and value of western criminology for teaching and practice in Trinidad and Tobago', in David Nelken (ed.), *Contrasting Criminal Justice*. Aldershot: Dartmouth. pp. 265–94.

Cain, Maureen (2000b) 'Orientalism, occidentalism and the sociology of crime', *British Journal of Criminology*, 40: 239–60.

Cain, Maureen and Howe, Adrian (eds) (2008) *Women, Crime and Social Harm*. Oxford: Hart Publishing.

Cavadino, Michael and Dignan James (2006a) 'Penal policy and political economy', *Criminology and Criminal Justice*, 6 (4): 435–56.

Cavadino, Michael and Dignan, James (2006b) *Penal Systems: A Comparative Approach*. London: Sage.

Clinard, Marshall B. (1978) *Cities with Little Crime*. Cambridge: Cambridge University Press.

Cohen, Albert (1970) 'Multiple factor approaches', in Marvin Wolfgang et al. (eds), *The Sociology of Crime and Delinquency*. New York: John Wiley. pp. 123–6.

Cohen, Stan (1972) *Folk Devils and Moral Panics*. Harmondsworth: Penguin.

Cohen, Stan (1985) *Visions of Social Control*. Cambridge: Polity Press.

Cole, George F., Frankowski, Stanislaw and Gertz, Marc G. (1987) *Major Criminal Justice Systems: A Comparative Survey*. Beverly Hills, CA: Sage.

Coombe, Rosemary J. (1998) 'Contingent articulations: a critical cultural studies of law', in Austin Sarat and Paul Kearns (eds), *Law in the Domains of Culture*. Ann Arbor, MI: University of Michigan Press. pp. 21–65.

Crawford, Adam (2000a) 'Contrasts in victim–offender mediation and appeals to community in France and the UK', in David Nelken (ed.), *Contrasting Criminal Justice*. Aldershot: Dartmouth. pp. 205–29.

Crawford, Adam (2000b) 'Why British criminologists lose their critical faculties upon crossing the English channel', *Social Work in Europe*, 7: 22–30.

Crawford, Adam (2010) 'From the shopping mall to the street corner', in Adam Crawford (ed.), *International and Comparative Criminal Justice and Urban Governance* Cambridge: Cambridge University Press.

Damaška, Mirjan R. (1986) *The Faces of Justice and State Authority*. New Haven, CT: Yale University Press.

Dammer, Harry R., Fairchild, Erika and Albanese, Jay S. (2005) *Comparative Criminal Justice*. Belmont, CA: Thomson.

Davies, John (2009) *How Albanian Women in France Use Trafficking to Overcome Social Exclusion (1998–2001)*. Amsterdam: University of Amsterdam Press.

De Georgi, Alessandro (2007) *Rethinking the Political Economy of Punishment*. Aldershot: Ashgate.

Deflem, Mathias (2002) *Policing World Society*. Cambridge: Cambridge University Press.

Della Porta, Donatella and Meny, Yves (eds) (1997) *Democracy and Corruption in Europe*. London: Pinter.

Delmas-Marty, Mirelle and Spencer, John R. (2002) *European Criminal Procedures*. Cambridge: Cambridge University Press.

Dembour, Marie-Bénédicte (2006) *Who Believes in Human Rights? Reflections on the European Convention*. Cambridge: Cambridge University Press.

Dezalay, Yves and Garth, Bryant (2002) *The Internationalisation of Palace Wars*. Chicago: University of Chicago Press.

Downes, David (1988) *Contrasts in Tolerance*. Oxford: Oxford University Press.

Downes, David (1990) 'Response to Herman Franke', *British Journal of Criminology*, 30 (1): 94–6.

Downes, David (2007) 'Visions of penal control in the Netherlands', in Michael Tonry (ed.), *Crime and Justice*. Vol. 36: *Crime, Punishment and Politics in Comparative Perspective*. Chicago: University of Chicago Press. pp. 93–127.

Downes, David (2010) 'Comparative criminology, globalisation and the "punitive turn"', in David Nelken (ed.), *Comparative Criminal Justice and Globalisation*. Aldershot: Ashgate.

Downes, David and Van Swaaningen, Renee (2007) 'The road to dystopia? Changes in the penal climate of the Netherlands', in Michael Tonry and Catrien Bijleveld (eds), *Crime and Justice in the Netherlands*. pp. 31–70.

Drake, Deborah, Muncie, John and Westmorland, Lousie (eds) (2010a) *Crime: Local and Global*. Milton Keynes: Open University Press.

Drake, Deborah, Muncie, John and Westmorland, Lousie (eds) (2010b) *Criminal Justice: Local and Global*. Milton Keynes: Open University Press.

Dyson, Kenneth (1980) *The State Tradition in Western Europe*. Oxford: Martin Robertson.

Edwards, Adam and Hughes, Gordon (2005) 'Comparing the governance of safety in Europe', *Theoretical Criminology*, 9 (3): 345–63.

Eliot, T. S. (1971) *Little Gidding*. New York: Minerva.

Estrada, Felipe (2006) 'Trends in violence in Scandinavia according to different indicators', *British Journal of Criminology*, 46 (3): 486–504.

Eve, Michael (1996) 'Comparing Italy: the case of corruption', in D. Forgacs and R. Lumley (eds), *Italian Cultural Studies: An Introduction*. Oxford: Oxford University Press. pp. 34–51.

Feeley, Malcolm (1983) *Court Reform on Trial: Why Simple Solutions Fail*. New York: Basic Books.

Feeley, Malcolm (1997) 'Comparative criminal law for criminologists: comparing for what purpose', in David Nelken (ed.), *Comparing Legal Cultures*. Aldershot: Ashgate. pp. 93–104.

Feeley, Malcolm and Simon, Jonathan (1994) 'Actuarial Justice: the emerging new criminal law', in David Nelken (ed.), *The Futures of Criminology*. London: Sage. pp. 173–201.

Fenwick, Mark (2005) 'Youth crime and crime control in contemporary Japan', in Colin Sumner (ed.), *Blackwell Handbook of Criminology*. Oxford: Blackwell. p. 125.

Ferrajoli, Luigi (1989) *Diritti e Ragione*. Rome: Laterza.

Ferrarese, Marie Rosarie (1997) 'An entrepreneurial conception of the law: the American model through Italian eyes', in David Nelken (ed.), *Comparing Legal Cultures*. Aldershot: Ashgate. p. 157.

Field, Stewart (2006) 'State, citizen and character in the French criminal process', *Journal of Law and Society*, 33 (4): 522–46.

Field, Stewart and Nelken, David (2007) 'Early intervention and the cultures of youth justice: a comparison of Italy and Wales', in Volkmar Gessner and David Nelken (eds), *European Ways of Law*. Oxford: Hart Publishing. pp. 349–74.

Fields, C.B. and Moore, R.H. (eds) (2005) *Comparative Criminal Justice*. Prospect Heights, IL: Waveland Press.

Findlay, Mark (2008) *Governing through Globalised Crime*. Cullompton: Willan Publishing.

Franke, Herman (1990) 'Dutch tolerance: facts and fables', *British Journal of Criminology*, 30: 81–93.

Frase, Richard S. (1990) 'Criminal justice as a guide to American law reform: how the French do it, how can we find out and why should we care?', *California Law Review*, 78: 539.

Friedman, Jonathan (1994) *Cultural Identity and Global Process*. London: Sage.

Friedman, Lawrence (1975) *The Legal System: A Social Science Perspective*. New York: Russell Sage.

Fukumi, Sayaka (2009) *Cocaine Trafficking in Latin America: EU and US Policy Response*. Aldershot: Ashgate.

Garland, David (1996) 'The limits of the sovereign state: strategies of crime control in contemporary society', *British Journal of Criminology*, 36: 445–71.

Garland, David (2001) *The Culture of Control*. Oxford: Oxford University Press.

Geertz, Clifford (1973) *Local Knowledge: Further Essays in Interpretive Anthropology*. New York: Basic Books.

Geertz, Clifford (1988) *Works and Lives*. Stanford, CA: Stanford University Press.

Gerber, Theodore P. and Mendelson, Sarah E. (2008) 'Public experiences of police violence and corruption in contemporary Russia: a case of predatory policing?', *Law & Society Review*, 42 (1): 1–44.

Goldstein, Abraham S. and Marcus, Martin (1977) 'The myth of judicial supervision in three "inquisitorial" systems: France, Italy, and Germany', *Yale Law Review*, 87: 240.

Gottschalk, Marie (2006) *The Prison and the Gallows: Mass Incarceration in America.* Cambridge: Cambridge University Press.

Grande, Elizabetta (2000) 'Italian criminal justice: borrowing and resistance', *American Journal of Comparative Law*, XLVIII: 227–60.

Green, David A. (2007) 'Comparing penal cultures: child-on-child homicide in England and Norway', in Michael Tonry (ed.), *Crime and Justice.* Vol. 36: *Crime, Punishment and Politics in a Comparative Perspective.* Chicago: University of Chicago Press. p. 591.

Greenberg, David and West, Vicki (2008) 'Siting the death penalty internationally', *Law & Social Inquiry*, 33: 295.

Haferkampf, H. and Ellis, H. (1992) 'Power, individualism and the sanctity of human life: development of criminality and punishment in four cultures', in H.G. Heiland, L.I. Shelley and H. Katoh (eds), *Crime and Control in Comparative Perspectives.* Berlin: De Gruyter. pp. 261–81.

Hagan, John and Wyland-Richmond, Fiona (2008) *Darfur and the Crime of Genocide.* Cambridge: Cambridge University Press.

Harcourt, Bernard (2006) *Against Prediction: Profiling, Policing, and Punishing in an Actuarial Age.* Chicago: University of Chicago Press.

Heidensohn, Frances (2006) 'Contrasts and concepts: considering the development of comparative criminology', in Tim Newburn and Paul Rock (eds), *The Politics of Crime Control.* Oxford: Oxford University Press. pp. 173–196.

Heidensohn, Frances (2007) 'International comparative research in criminology', in Roy D. King and Emma Winkup (eds), *Doing Research on Crime and Justice.* Oxford: Oxford University Press. 199–230.

Hinds, Lyn (2005) 'Crime control in western countries, 1970–2000', in John Pratt et al. (eds), *The New Punitiveness.* Cullompton: Willan Publishing. p. 47.

Hodgson, Jaqueline (2005) *French Criminal Justice.* Oxford: Hart Publishing.

Hofstede, Gert (1980) *Culture's Consequences.* London: Sage.

Honoré, Carl (2004) *In Praise of Slow.* London: Orion.

Hood, Roger (2001) 'The death penalty: a worldwide perspective', *Punishment and Society*, 3: 331–54 .

Hughes, Graham (1984) 'English Criminal Justice: is it better than ours?', *Arizona Law Review*, 26: 507.

Johnson, David (2000) 'Prosecutor culture in Japan and USA', in David Nelken (ed.), *Contrasting Criminal Justice.* Aldershot: Dartmouth. pp. 157–204.

Johnson, David (2001) *The Japanese Way of Justice.* Oxford: Oxford University Press.

Johnson, David (2003) 'Police integrity in Japan', in Carl Klockars et al. (eds), *The Contours of Police Integrity.* London: Sage. p. 130.

Johnson, David and Zimring, Frank (2008) *The Next Frontier? National Development, Human Rights, and the Death Penalty in Asia.* New York: Oxford University Press.

Jones, Trevor and Newburn, Tim (2008) *Policy Transfer and Criminal Justice.* Milton Keynes: Open University Press.

Junger-Tas, Josine and Decker, Scott (eds) (2006) *International Handbook of Juvenile Justice*. New York: Springer.

Karstedt, Susanne (2002) 'Durkheim, Tarde and beyond: the global travel of crime policies', *Criminology and Criminal Justice*, 2 (2): 111–23.

Karstedt, Susanne (2008) 'Comparing cultures, comparing crime: challenges, prospects and problems for a global criminology', in Nick Larsen and Russell Smandych (eds), *Global Criminology and Criminal Justice: Current Issues and Perspectives*. Buffalo, NY: Broadview Press. p. 23.

Killias, Martin (1989) 'Book review of Balvig', *British Journal of Criminology*, 29: 300–5.

Klockars, Carl B., Ivkovich, Sanja Kutnjak and Haberfeld, Maria R. (eds) (2004) *The Contours of Police Integrity*. London: Sage.

Krisberg, Barry (2006) 'Rediscovering the juvenile justice ideal in the United States', in John Muncie and Barry Goldson (eds), *Comparative Youth Justice: Critical Issues*. London: Sage. p. 6.

Lacey, Nicola (2008) *The Prisoners' Dilemma: Political Economy and Punishment in Contemporary Democracies*. Cambridge: Cambridge University Press.

Lacey, Nicola and Zedner, Lucia (1998) 'Community in German criminal justice: a significant absence?', *Social and Legal Studies*, 7 (1): 7–25.

Langbein, John H. and Weinreb, Lloyd (1978) 'Continental criminal procedure: myth and reality', *Law Journal*, 87 (8): 1549.

Lappi-Seppala, Tapoio (2007) 'Penal policy in Scandinavia', in Michael Tonry (ed.), *Crime and Justice*. Vol. 36: *Crime, Punishment and Politics in Comparative Perspective*. Chicago: University of Chicago Press. pp. 217–95.

Larsen, Nick and Smandych, Russell (eds) (2008) *Global Criminology and Criminal Justice: Current Issues and Perspectives*. Buffalo, NY: Broadview Press.

Lasser, Mitchell (2005) 'The European pasteurization of French law', *Cornell Law Review*, 90: 995–1083.

Lazarus, Liora (2004) *Contrasting Prisoners' Rights: A Comparative Examination of England and Germany*. Oxford: Oxford University Press.

Leavitt, Geoffrey C. (1990/1997) 'Relativism and cross-cultural criminology: a critical analysis', reprinted in Piers Beirne and David Nelken (eds), *Issues in Comparative Criminology*. Aldershot: Dartmouth. pp. 25–50.

Lemert, Edwin (1986) 'Juvenile Justice: Italian style', *Law and Society Review*, 20: 309–44.

Lévy, René (2007) 'Pardons and amnesties as policy instruments in contemporary France', in Michael Tonry (ed.), *Crime and Justice*. Vol. 36: *Crime, Punishment and Politics in Comparative Perspective*. Chicago: University of Chicago Press. p. 551.

Lind, Edgar A. and Tyler, Tom (1988) *The Social Psychology of Procedural Justice*. New York: Plenum Press.

Loader, Ian (2006) ' The fall of the "Platonic Guardians": liberalism, criminology and political responses to crime in England and Wales', *British Journal of Criminology*, 46 (4): 561–86.

Loader, Ian and Walker, Neil (2007) *Civilizing Security*. Cambridge: Cambridge University Press.

Macrudden, Robert (2007) 'Judicial comparativism and human rights', in Esin Orucu and David Nelken (eds), *Comparative Law: A Handbook*. Oxford: Hart Publishing. p. 371.

Markovits, Inga (1995) *Imperfect Justice: An East–West German Diary*. Oxford: Oxford University Press.

Mathews, Roger (2005) 'The myth of punitiveness', *Theoretical Criminology*, 9 (2): 175–201.

Mawby, Robert I. and Kirchoff, Gerd (1996) 'Coping with crime: a comparison of victims' experiences in England and Germany', in Pamela Davies, Peter Francis and Victor Jupp (eds), *Understanding Victimisation: Themes and Perspectives*. Newcastle: University of Northumbria Press. pp. 55–70.

Melossi, Dario (1990) *The State of Social Control*. Oxford: Polity Press.

Melossi, Dario (1994) 'The "economy" of illegalities: normal crimes, elites and social control in comparative analysis', in David Nelken (ed.), *The Futures of Criminology*. London: Sage. pp. 202–19.

Melossi, Dario (2001) 'The cultural embeddedness of social control: reflections on the comparison of Italian and North American cultures concerning punishment', *Theoretical Criminology*, 5: 403–24.

Merry, Sally E. (2006) *Human Rights and Gender Violence: Translating International Law into Local Justice*. Chicago: University of Chicago Press.

Miyazawa, Setsuo (2008) 'The politics of increasing punitiveness and the rising populism in Japanese criminal justice policy', *Punishment and Society*, 10 (1): 47–77.

Mohr, Richard and Contini, Francesco (2008) 'Judicial evaluation in context: principles, practices and promise in nine European countries', *European Journal of Legal Studies*, 1: 2.

Montana, Riccardo and Nelken, David (forthcoming) 'Prosecution, legal culture and resistance to moral panics in Italy', in Cindy Smith, Sheldon Zhang and Rosemary Barberet (eds), *Handbook of International Criminology*. London: Routledge.

Morgan, Rod (2000) 'Developing prison standards compared', *Punishment and Society*, 2 (3): 325–42 .

Morrison, Wayne (2004) 'Criminology, genocide and modernity: remarks on the companion that criminology ignored', in Colin Sumner (ed.), *Blackwell Handbook of Criminology*. Oxford: Blackwell. p. 68.

Muncie, John (2005) 'The globalization of crime control – the case of youth and juvenile justice: neo-liberalism, policy convergence and international conventions', *Theoretical Criminology*, 9 (1): 35–64.

Muncie, John and Goldson, Barry (eds) (2006) *Comparative Youth Justice: Critical Issues*. London: Sage.

Munro, Vanessa (2006) 'Stopping traffic? A comparative study of responses to the trafficking in women for prostitution', *British Journal of Criminology*, 46 (2): 318–33.

Naim, Moses (2005) *Illicit: How Smugglers Traffickers and Copycats are Hijacking the Global Economy*. New York: Arrow Books.

Nelken, David (1984) 'Law in action or living law? Back to the beginning in sociology of law', *Legal Studies*, 4: 152–74.

Nelken, David (1992/1996) 'Law and disorder in Italy', reprinted in Volkmar Gessner, Armin Hoeland and Csaba Varga (eds), *European Legal Cultures*. Aldershot: Dartmouth. pp. 335–8.

Nelken, David (1993) 'Le giustificazioni della pena ed i diritti dell'imputato', in Letizia Gianformaggio (ed.), *Le Ragioni del Garantismo*. Turin: Giappicheli. pp. 275–307.

Nelken, David (1994a) 'Reflexive criminology?', in David Nelken (ed.), *The Futures of Criminology*. London: Sage. pp. 7–43.

Nelken, David (1994b) 'Whom can you trust? The future of comparative criminology', in David Nelken (ed.), *The Futures of Criminology*. London: Sage. pp. 220–44.

Nelken, David (1996) 'Judicial politics and corruption in Italy', in Michael Levi and David Nelken (eds), *The Corruption of Politics and the Politics of Corruption*. Special issue of the *Journal of Law and Society*: 355–58.

Nelken, David (1997a) *Comparing Legal Cultures*. Aldershot: Dartmouth.

Nelken, David (1997b) 'Il significato di Tangentopoli: la risposta giudiziaria alla corruzione e i suoi limiti', in Luciano Violante (ed.), *Storia d'Italia 14: Legge, Diritto e Giustizia*. Turin: Einaudi. pp. 597–627.

Nelken, David (1997c) 'The globalization of crime and criminal justice: prospects and problems', in Michael Freeman (ed.), *Law and Opinion at the end of the 20th Century*. Oxford: Oxford University Press. pp. 251–79.

Nelken, David (ed.) (2000a) *Contrasting Criminal Justice*. Aldershot: Ashgate.

Nelken, David (2000b) 'Telling difference: of crime and criminal justice in Italy', in David Nelken (ed.), *Contrasting Criminal Justice*. Aldershot: Ashgate. pp. 233–64.

Nelken, David (2002) 'Comparing criminal justice', in Michael Maguire, Rod Morgan and Robert Reiner (eds), *Oxford Handbook of Criminology* (3rd edn). Oxford: Oxford University Press. pp. 175–202.

Nelken, David (2003a) 'Criminology: crime's changing boundaries', in Peter Cane and Mark Tushnet (eds), *The Oxford Handbook of Legal Studies*. Oxford: Oxford University Press. pp. 250–70.

Nelken, David (2003b) 'Corruption in the European Union', in Martin Bull and James Newell (eds), *Corruption and Scandal in Contemporary Politics*. London: Macmillan. pp. 220–33.

Nelken, David (2004a) 'Using the concept of legal culture', *Australian Journal of Legal Philosophy*, 29: 1–28.

Nelken, David (2004b) 'Being there', in Lin Chao and John Winterdyk (eds), *Lessons from International/Comparative Criminology/Criminal Justice*. Toronto: De Sitter. pp. 83–92.

Nelken, David (2005) 'When is a society non-punitive? A case study of Italy', in John Pratt et al. (eds), *The New Punitiveness*. Cullompton: Willan Publishing. pp. 218–38.

Nelken, David (2006a) 'Il radicamento della penalità', in Alberto Febbrajo, Antonio La Spina and Monica Raiteri (eds), *Cultura Giuridica e Politiche Pubbliche*. Milan: Giuffré. pp. 200–35.

Nelken, David (2006b) 'Italy: a lesson in tolerance?', in John Muncie and Barry Goldson (eds), *Comparative Youth Justice: Critical Issues*. London: Sage. pp. 159–76.

Nelken, David (2006c) 'Italian juvenile justice: tolerance, leniency or indulgence?', *Youth Justice*, 6: 107–28.

Nelken, David (2006d) 'Rethinking legal culture', in Michael Freeman (ed.), *Law and Sociology*. Oxford: Oxford University Press. pp. 200–24.

Nelken, David (2006e) 'Patterns of punishment', *Modern Law Review*, 69: 262–77.

Nelken, David (2006f) 'Signaling conformity: changing norms in Japan and China', *Michigan Journal of International Law*, 27: 933–72.

Nelken, David (2007a) 'Comparative law and comparative legal studies', in Esin Orucu and David Nelken (eds), *Comparative Law: A Handbook*. Oxford: Hart Publishing. pp. 3–42.

Nelken, David (2007b) 'Three problems in studying legal culture', in Freek Bruinsma and David Nelken (eds), *Exploring Legal Cultures*. Special issue of *Recht der Werkelijkheid*, 28: 11–28.

Nelken, David (2007c) 'Immigrant beach selling along the Italian Adriatic coast: de-constructing a social problem', in Paul Ponsaers and Ronnie Lippens (eds), *The Informal Economy Re-visited: Organisational Process, Occupational Culture, Informal Economies, and Crime*. Special issue of *Crime, Law and Social Change*, 297–313.

Nelken, David (2008) 'Normalising time: European integration and court delays in Italy', in Hanne Petersen, Helle Krunke, Anne-Lise Kjær and Mikael Rask Madsen (eds), *Paradoxes of European Integration*. Aldershot: Ashgate. pp. 299–323.

Nelken, David (2009a) 'Corruption as governance', in Franz von Benda-Beckmann and Keebet von Benda-Beckmann (eds), *Rules of Law, Laws of Ruling*. Aldershot: Ashgate. pp. 275–95.

Nelken, David (2009b) 'Comparing criminal justice: beyond ethnocentrism and relativism'. *European Journal of Criminology*, 6 (4): 291–311.

Nelken, David (2009c) *Beyond the Law in Context*. Aldershot: Ashgate.

Nelken, David (2010) 'Making sense of difference', in Shlomo Shoham, Paul Knepper and Martin Kett (eds), *International Handbook of Criminology*. London: Taylor and Francis. pp. 60–80.

Nelken, David (forthcoming a) 'Legal culture and human trafficking', paper presented at the conference on the Palermo protocol, Palermo, May 2009.

Nelken, David (forthcoming b) 'Traveling concepts: prison rules and corruption standards', Public lecture at Institute of Advanced Studies, Oxford Centre of Criminology and Utrecht Law School, Spring 2009.

Nelken, David and Maneri, Marcello (2000) 'La produzione della notizia giudiziaria e il segreto investigativo. Un'indagine sociologica', in Glauco Giostra (ed.), *Proceedings of a National Research Project into Legal Delay*. Place. Macerata Institute of Criminal Procedure. pp. 213–91.

Nelken, David and Zanier, Letizia (2006) 'Tra norma e prassi: durata del processo e strategie degli operatori del diritto', *Sociologia del Diritto*, 2006: 143–66.

Newburn, Tim (2006) 'Contrasts in intolerance: the culture of control in the United States and Britain', in Tim Newburn and Paul Rock (eds), *The Politics of Crime Control*. Oxford: Oxford University Press. pp. 227–70.

Newburn, Tim and Sparks, Richard (2004) *Criminal Justice and Political Cultures: National and International Dimensions of Crime Control*. Cullompton: Willan Publishing. pp. 80–103.

Newman, Graeme (1999) *Global Report on Crime and Justice*. Oxford: Oxford University Press.

Nolan, Jim L. (2009) *Legal Accents, Legal Borrowing: The International Problem-solving Court Movement*. Princeton, NJ: Princeton University Press.

O'Malley, Pat (1999) 'Volatile and contradictory punishment', *Theoretical Criminology*, 3: 175–96.

O'Sullivan, Eoin and O'Donnell, Ian (2007) 'Coercive confinement in the republic of Ireland: the waning of a culture of control', *Punishment and Society*, 9 (1): 27–48.

Packer, Herbert (1964) 'Two models of the criminal process', *University of Pennsylvania Law Review*, 113 (1): 1–68.

Pakes, Francis (2004) *Comparative Criminal Justice*. Cullompton: Willan Publishing.

Passas, Nikos and Nelken, David (1993) 'The thin line between legitimate and criminal enterprises: subsidy frauds in the European Community', *Crime, Law and Social Change*, 19: 223–43.

Pavarini, Massimo (1997) 'Questions and answers about security in Italy at the end of the millenium', in Roberto Bergalli and Colin Sumner (eds), *Social Control and Political Order*. London: Sage. p. 75.

Pease, Ken (1994) 'Cross-national imprisonment rates: limitations of method and possible conclusions', in Roy King and Michael Maguire (eds), *Prison in Context*. Oxford: Oxford University Press. pp. 116–30.

Pizzi, William T. (1999) *Trials without Truth: Why Our System of Criminal Trials Has Become an Expensive Failure*. New York: New York University Press.

Polak, Paolina and Nelken, David (2010) 'Polish prosecutors, corruption and legal culture', in Alberto Febbrajo and Woijech Sadurski (eds), *East-Central Europe After Transition: Towards a New Socio-legal Semantics*. Aldershot: Ashgate.

Pound, Roscoe (1910) 'Law in books and law in action', *New York Law Review*, 44: 12.

Pratt, John, Brown, David, Hallsworth, Simon, Brown, Mark and Morrison, Wayne (eds) (2005) *The New Punitiveness*. Cullompton: Willan Publishing.

Reichel, Phillip L. (2007) *Handbook of Transnational Crime and Justice* (4th edn). New York: Sage.

Reichel, Phillip L. (2008) *Comparative Criminal Justice Systems* (5th edn). Upper Saddle River, NJ: Prentice-Hall.

Roach, Kent (1998) 'Four models of the criminal process', *Journal of Criminal Law and Criminology*, 9: 671.

Roberts, Julian and Hough, J.M. (2005) *Understanding Public Attitudes to Criminal Justice*. Milton Keynes: Open University Press.

Roberts, Paul (2002) 'On method: the ascent of comparative criminal justice', *Oxford Journal of Legal Studies*, 22 (3): 529–61.

Roche, Sebastian (2007) 'Criminal justice policy in France: illusions of severity', in Michael Tonry (ed.), *Crime and Justice*. Vol. 36: *Crime, Punishment and Politics in Comparative Perspective*. Chicago: University of Chicago Press. p. 471.

Rock, Paul (1986) *A View from the Shadows*. Oxford: Clarendon Press.

Ross, Jacqueline E. (2004) 'Impediments to transnational cooperation in undercover policing: a comparative study of the United States and Italy', *American Journal of Comparative Law*, 52 (3): 569–624.

Ross, Jaqueline E. (2007) 'The place of covert policing in democratic societies: a comparative study of the United States and Germany', *American Journal of Comparative Law*, 55: 493.

Roversi, Antonio (2008) *Hate on the Net*. Aldershot: Ashgate.

Ruggiero, Vincenzo (1996) *Organised and Corporate Crime in Europe: Offers that Can't Be Refused*. Aldershot: Dartmouth.

Ryan, Mick (2003) *Penal Policy and Political Cultures in England and Wales*. Winchester: Waterside.

Sarzotti, Claudio (2008) *Processi di selezione del crimine: Procure della Repubblica e organizzazione giudiziaria*. Milan: Giuffre.

Savelsberg, Joachim (1994) 'Knowledge, domination and criminal punishment', *American Journal of Sociology*, 99: 911–43.

Savelsberg, Joachim (1999) 'Knowledge domination and punishment revisited: incorporating state socialism', *Social Problems*, 1: 45–70.

Savelsberg, Joachim (2010) 'Globalization and states of punishment', in David Nelken (ed.), *Comparative Criminal Justice and Globalisation*. Aldershot: Ashgate.

Savelsberg, Joachim and King, Ryan (2005) 'Institutionalizing collective memories of hate: law and law enforcement in Germany and the United States', *American Journal of Sociology*, 111 (2): 579–61.

Savelsberg, Joachim, King, Ryan and Cleveland, Lara (2002) 'Politicized scholarship? Science on crime and the state', *Social Problems*, 49 (3): 327–48.

Shapiro, Martin (1981) *Courts*. Chicago: University of Chicago Press.

Sheptycki, Jim (2002) *In Search of Transnational Policing*. Aldershot: Ashgate.

Sheptycki, Jim and Wardak, Ali (2005) *Transnational and Comparative Criminology*. London: Glasshouse Press.

Sherman, Larry W. et al. (eds) (1997) *Preventing Crime: What Works, What Doesn't, What's Promising*. Report to the US Congress. Washington, DC: US Dept.

Simon, Jonathan (2007) *Governing through Crime*. Oxford: Oxford University Press.

Solivetti, Luigi (2010) *Immigration, Integration and Crime: A Cross-national Approach*. London: Routledge.

Szabo, Dennis (1975) 'Comparative criminology', *Journal of Criminal Law and Criminology*, 66: 366–79.

Sztompka, Piotr (1990) 'Conceptual frameworks in comparative inquiry: divergent or convergent', in Martin Albrow and Elizabeth King (eds), *Globalization, Knowledge and Society*. London: Sage. p. 47.

Tonry, Michael (1995) *Malign Neglect: Race Crime and Punishment in America*. New York: Oxford University Press.

Tonry, Michael (2001) 'Symbol, substance, and severity in western penal policies', *Punishment and Society*, 3 (4): 517.

Tonry, Michael (2005) 'Why are Europe's crime rates falling?', *ESRC Newsletter*, July: 8.

Tonry, Michael (2007a) 'Introduction', in Michael Tonry (ed.), *Crime and Justice*. Vol. 36: *Crime, Punishment and Politics in Comparative Perspective*. Chicago: University of Chicago Press. p. 1.

Tonry, Michael (ed.) (2007b) *Crime and Justice*. Vol. 36: *Crime, Punishment and Politics in Comparative Perspective*. Chicago: University of Chicago Press.

Travers, Max (2008) 'Understanding comparison in criminal justice research: an interpretive perspective', *International Criminal Justice Review*, 18 (4): 389–405.

Twining, William (2005) 'Have concepts, will travel: analytical jurisprudence in a global context', *International Journal of Law in Context*, 1 (1): 5.

Vagg, John (1993) 'Context and linkage: reflections on comparative research and "internationalism" in criminology', *British Journal of Criminology*, 33: 541–54.

Van Dijk, Jan (2007) *The World of Crime*. London: Sage.

Van Dijk, Jan, Van Kesteren, John, Smit, Paul, Tilburg University, UNICRI and UNODC (2007) *Criminal Victimisation in International Perspective: Key Findings from the 2004–2005 ICVS and EU ICS*. The Hague: Ministry of Justice, WODC.

Van Hofer, Hanns (2003) 'Prison populations as political constructs: the case of Finland, Holland and Sweden', *Journal of Scandinavian Studies in Criminology and Crime Prevention*, 4 (1): 21–38.

Van Schendel, Willem and Abraham, Itty (eds) (2005) *Illicit Flows and Criminal Things*. Bloomington, IN: Indiana University Press.

Van Swaaningen, René (1997) *Critical Criminology: Visions from Europe*. London: Sage.

Vogler, Richard (2005) *A World View of Criminal Justice*. Aldershot: Ashgate.

Volkmann-Schluck, Thomas (1981) 'Continental European criminal procedures: true or illusive model?', *American Journal of Criminal Law*, 9: 1.

Walmsley, Roy (1999) *World Prison List*. Available at: apcca.org.

Walmsley, Roy (2008) *World Prison List*. Available at: apcca.org.

Wandall, Rasmus H. (2006) 'Equality by numbers or words', *Criminal Law Forum*, 17 (1): 1–41.

Waquant, Loic (2009a) *Prisons of Poverty*. Minneappolis, MN: University of Minnesota Press.

Waquant, Loic (2009b) *Punishing the Poor: The Neoliberal Government of Social Insecurity*. Durham, NC: Duke University Press.

West, Mark D. (2009) *Secrets, Sex and Spectacle*. Chicago: University of Chicago Press.

Whitman, Jim Q. (2003) *Harsh Justice: Criminal Punishment and the Widening Divide between America and Europe*. Oxford: Oxford University Press.

Wilkinson, Richard (1996) *Unhealthy Societies: The Afflictions of Inequality*. London: Routledge.

Winterdyk, John and Cao, Liqun (2004) *Lessons from International/Comparative Criminology/Criminal Justice*. Toronto: De Sitter.

Winterson, Jeanette (1991) *Oranges Are Not the Only Fruit*. London: Vintage.

Wood, David Murakami (2009) 'The "Surveillance Society": questions of history, place and culture', *European Journal of Criminology*, 6 (2): 179–94.

Young, Jock (1988) 'Radical criminology in Britain: the emergence of a competing paradigm', *British Journal of Criminology*, 28 (2): 159.

Young, Jock (1999) *The Exclusive Society*. London: Sage.

Zedner, Lucia (1995) 'In pursuit of the vernacular: comparing law and order discourse in Britain and Germany', *Social and Legal Studies*, 517–34.

Zedner, Lucia (1996) 'German criminal justice culture', unpublished paper presented at the Onati Workshop on Changing Legal Cultures, Onati: Spain. 13–14 July.

Zedner, Lucia (2002) 'Dangers of dystopias in penal theory', *Oxford Journal of Legal Studies*, 22 (2): 341–66.

Zedner, Lucia (2003) 'The concept of security: an agenda for comparative analysis', *Legal Studies*, 23 (1): 167.

Zimring, Franklin E. (2006) 'The necessity and value of transnational comparative study: some preaching from a recent convert', *Criminology and Public Policy*, 5 (4): 615–22.

index

Page references in **bold** indicate tables.